NATURE Inspired

WINTER

2015

Nature Inspired: Winter Edition 2015

Published by Falling Leaves Press, Poughkeepsie, New York

Cover Image: Jan Töve, Signs #9, 2012, Photograph

Cover Design: Christine Agro
Concept: Christine Agro
Layout: Falling Leaves Press
www.fallingleavespress.com
info@fallingleavespress.com

Paperback
ISBN-10: 0-9970660-0-8
ISBN-13: 978-0-9970660-0-5

Falling Leaves Press

May you always see beauty.

Meet The Artists

Nature Inspired: Winter 2015 brings together a collection of art and writing by 40 artists from around the world.

Please come meet them at www.natureinspiredanthologies.com and find out more about their work as well as how to contact them.

Editor's Reflection

Winter can be seen as a stark, dull time in our lives. The days are shorter and colder. The vibrant pops of color are all gone, the trees are bare and we are left with shades of white, grey, brown and black.

I hear many people speak of winter with dread. At the first sign of winter coming, there is already a desire for it to be gone.

Between the pages of this book it is my hope that you will discover or will be reminded of the beauty that is winter, from crisp lines to whites so cold they look blue. It is my hope that you will be inspired to dig deep, to use the canvas of winter to soul search, to explore, to see the world with new eyes.

Many thanks to the artists whose works are within this edition. I thank them for their passion, their talent and their willingness to offer us an opportunity to see, feel, hear and explore winter in so many different ways.

As you make your way through the works in this edition may you be inspired to embrace this amazing season of sharp contrast and long shadows and may you take some time to reflect on the beauty and wonder that is winter.

Christine Agro

NATURE Inspired

WINTER

2015

Cover Image

Jan Töve

Signs #9

Photograph
30.46" x 40.9"

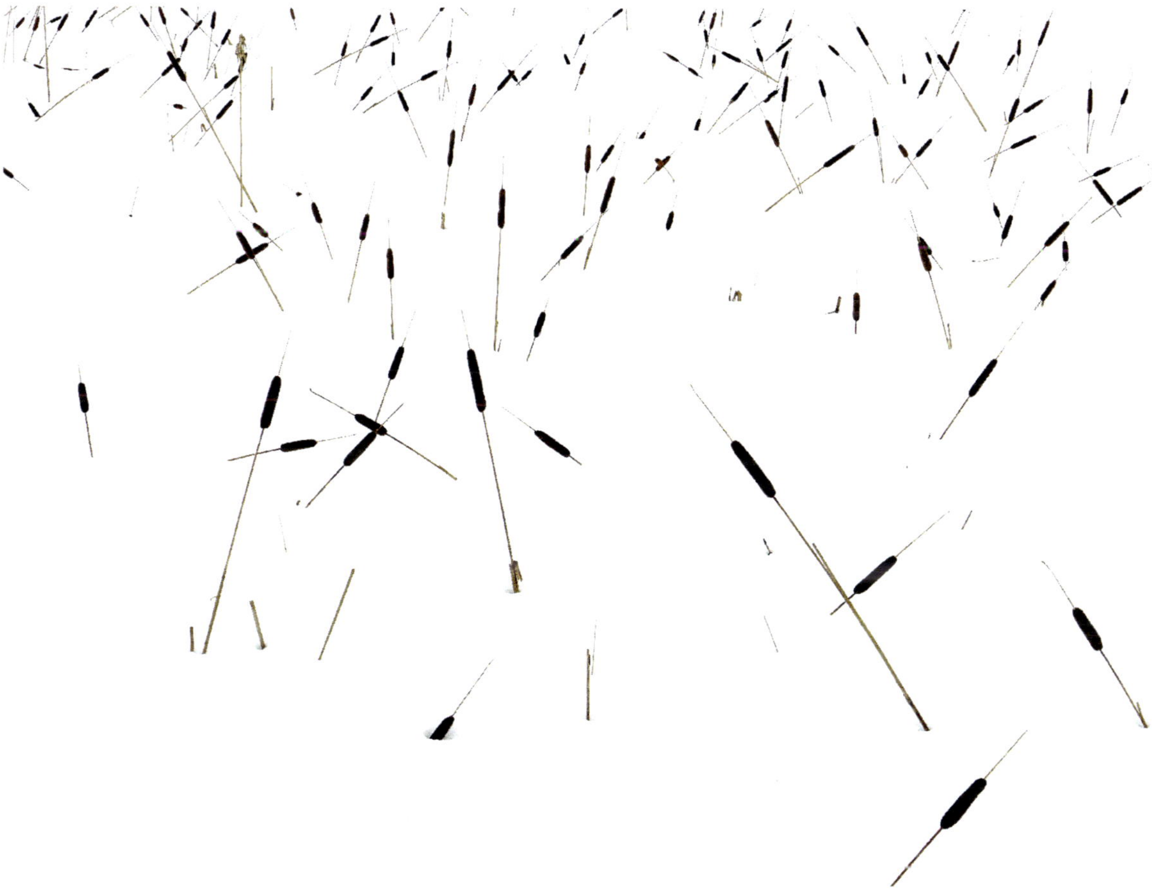

Jan Töve

Beech in Snow

Photograph

53.86" x 43.09"

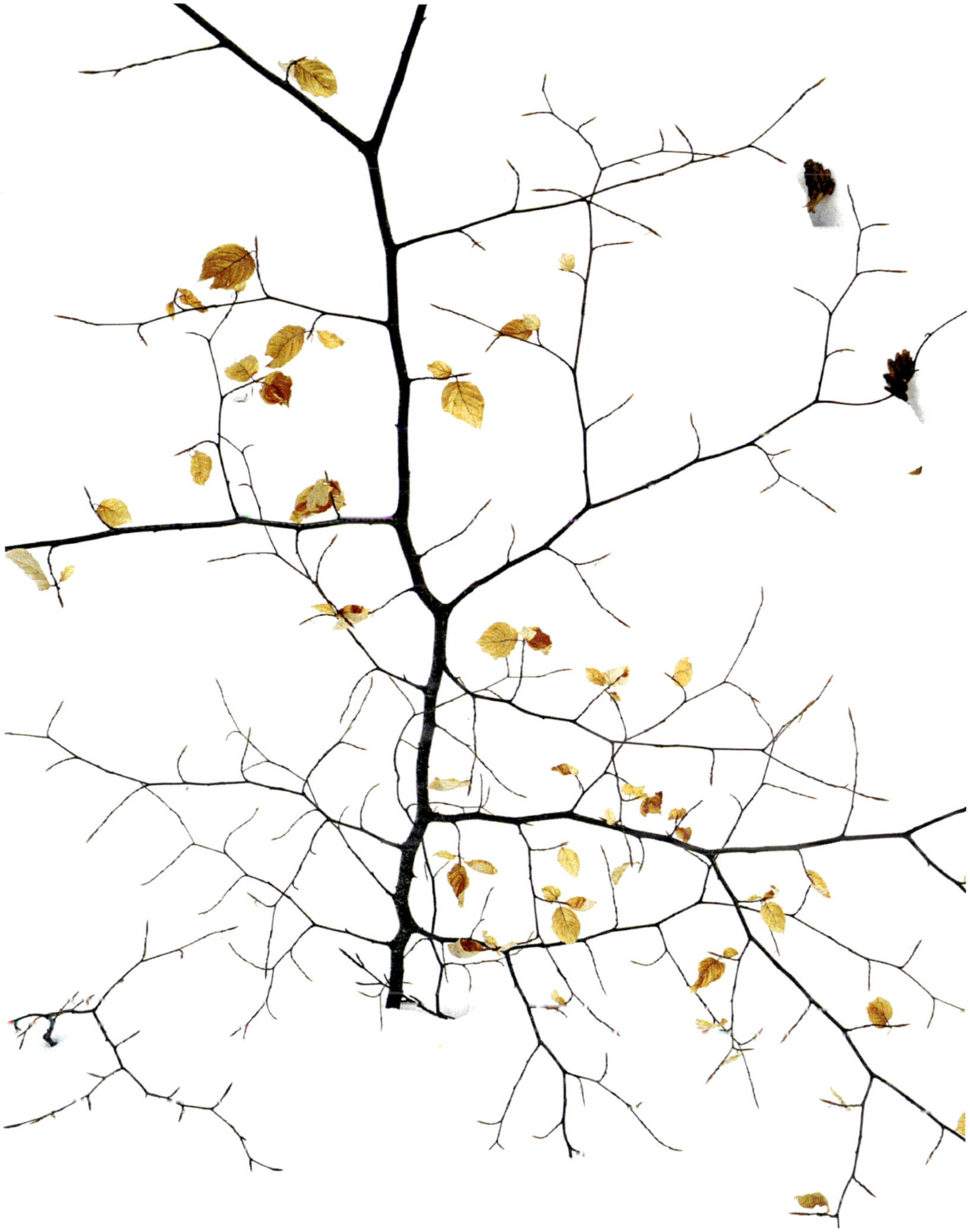

Jan Töve

The First Snowfall

Photograph

23.7" x 42.33"

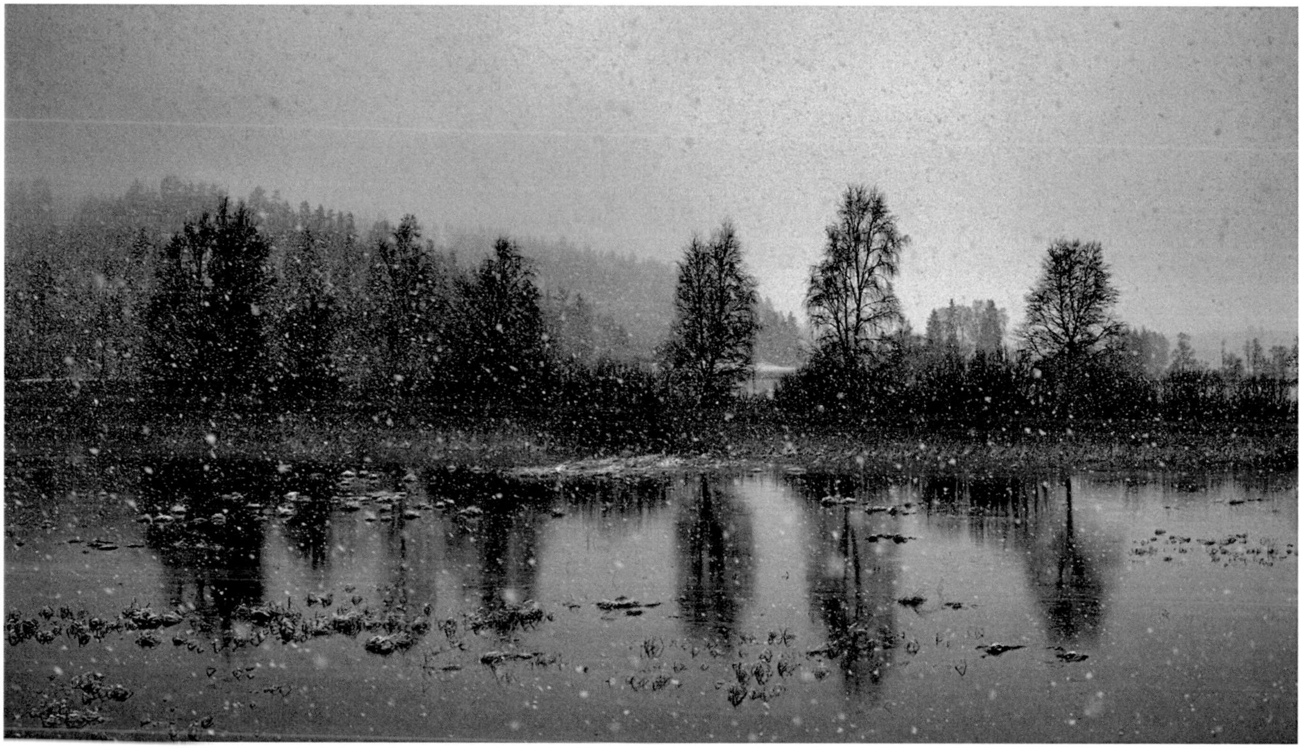

Waiting for the Light

By Jan Töve

Snowflakes fell and landed on your eyelashes. Melted. Moistened your cheek like tears. You smiled and broke from my embrace. Your pupils narrowed at the brightness of the winter landscape. A flock of redpolls flew up from the willow scrub and whirled away over the woods. We high-stepped through the snow to the big rock by the lake shore where we bathed in summer. Along the shore now was a low ridge of shiny ice - as if summer's last wave had frozen when it reached land.

We spread out a groundsheet and pulled out a thermos. Bulrushes stuck up through the ice like burnt-out New Year's rockets. I smiled at the memory of the time just after we had moved in when we picked a big bunch of them and put them in a pewter pot by the fireplace. After a few days in the warm room, they exploded and filled the whole apartment with fluffy seeds. It felt as if you read my mind when you pointed at them and said:
"Remember?"
I nodded. Then we burst out laughing.

There is a primeval force in the unseen. Concealed from our eyes, life bides its time waiting for the spring explosion. Seeds will germinate, eggs will hatch; larvae, pupas, tadpoles. In the dark, everything is set to go. In every cell a promise vibrates. In every bud a leaf awaits. Winter is just a hiatus. A breathing space while waiting for the light to return and water molecules to dance. Under the snow and ice, life lies dormant. In every cold body beats a warm heart. A slow pulse pumping towards the future, towards hope and survival. And belief in new opportunities - once again.

The snow has stopped. We pack away our stuff and get up. Brush each other off, wriggle into our rucksacks and start walking home in the fading light. You first and me behind. You suddenly stop mid-step and remain motionless.

"What is it?"

"Come. Quick." You yank my hand out of my jacket pocket and quickly put it under your sweater.

Silence. Not a breeze. Not a sound. Everything stands still. Time takes a break. Pauses and deliberates, balances on the very edge of a snow-lit day. I hear you whisper "Feel it?" when my hand is touched by a quick movement, a small kick. I give a start. Our eyes meet. The snow begins to fall again, lands on our eyelashes. Melts. And runs down our cheeks. I put out my tongue to lick a drop. This time it tastes salty.

Ilkka Volanen

Koppelo Ice, 2015
Photograph
9.5 in x 14 in

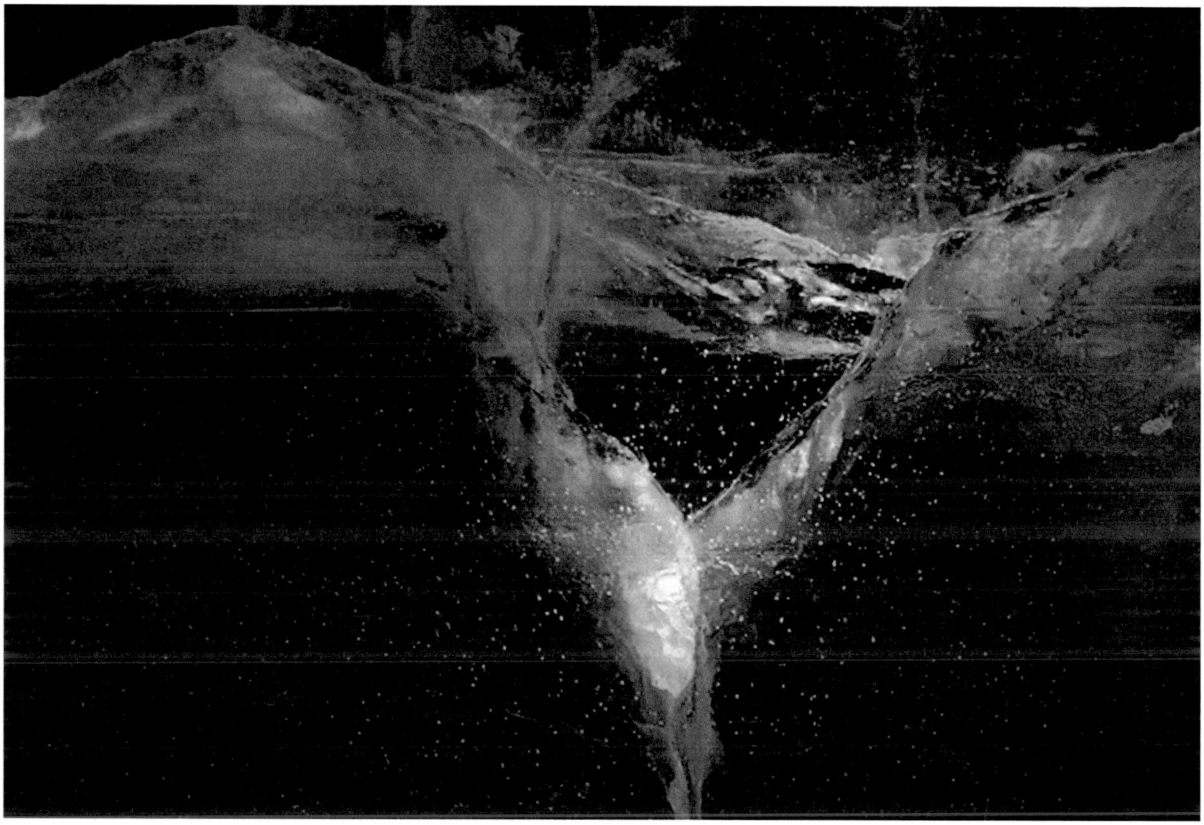

Ilkka Volanen

Koppelo Landscape 2

Photograph

24 in x 36in

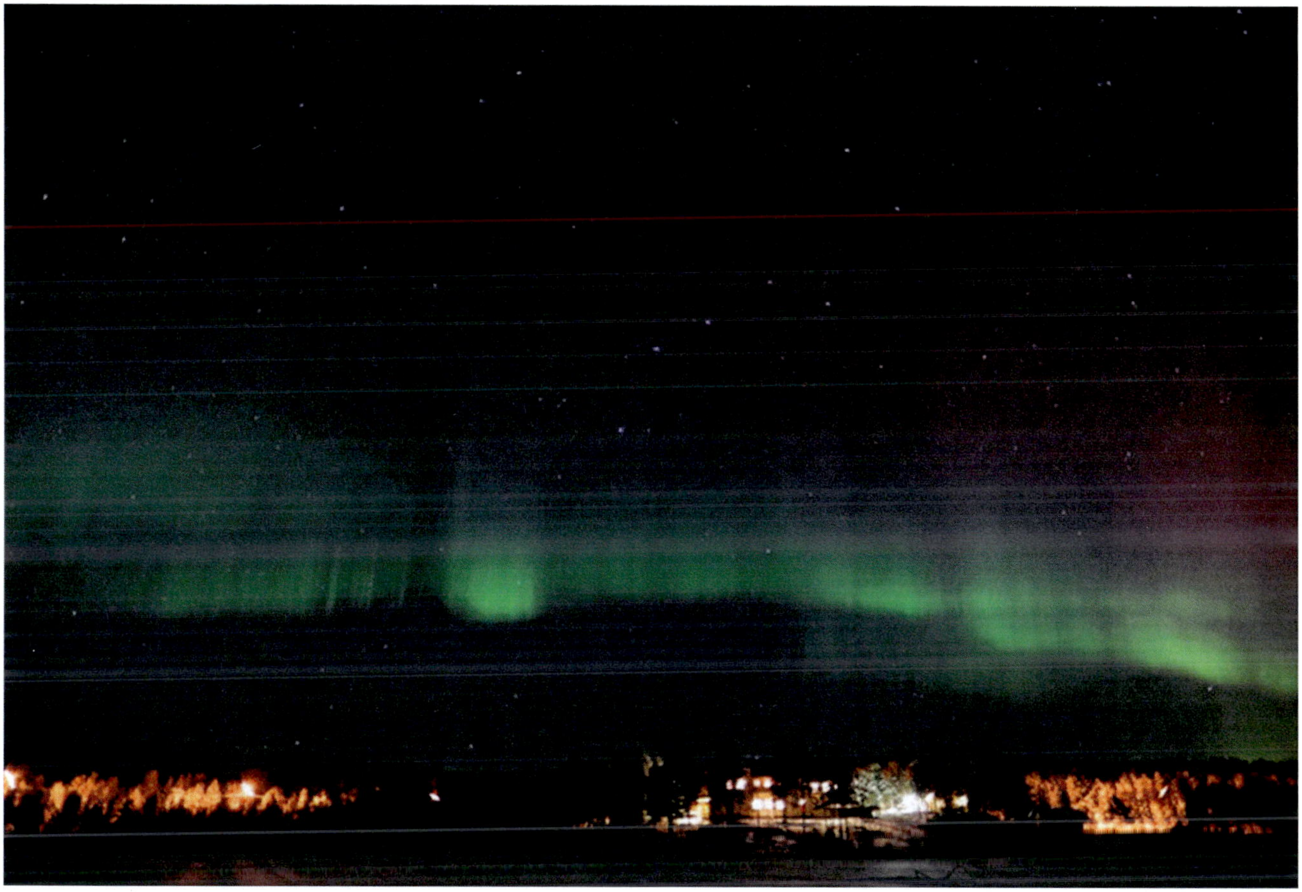

Matt Frieburghaus

Icebergs, 2015

Digital Print

30 in x 38 in

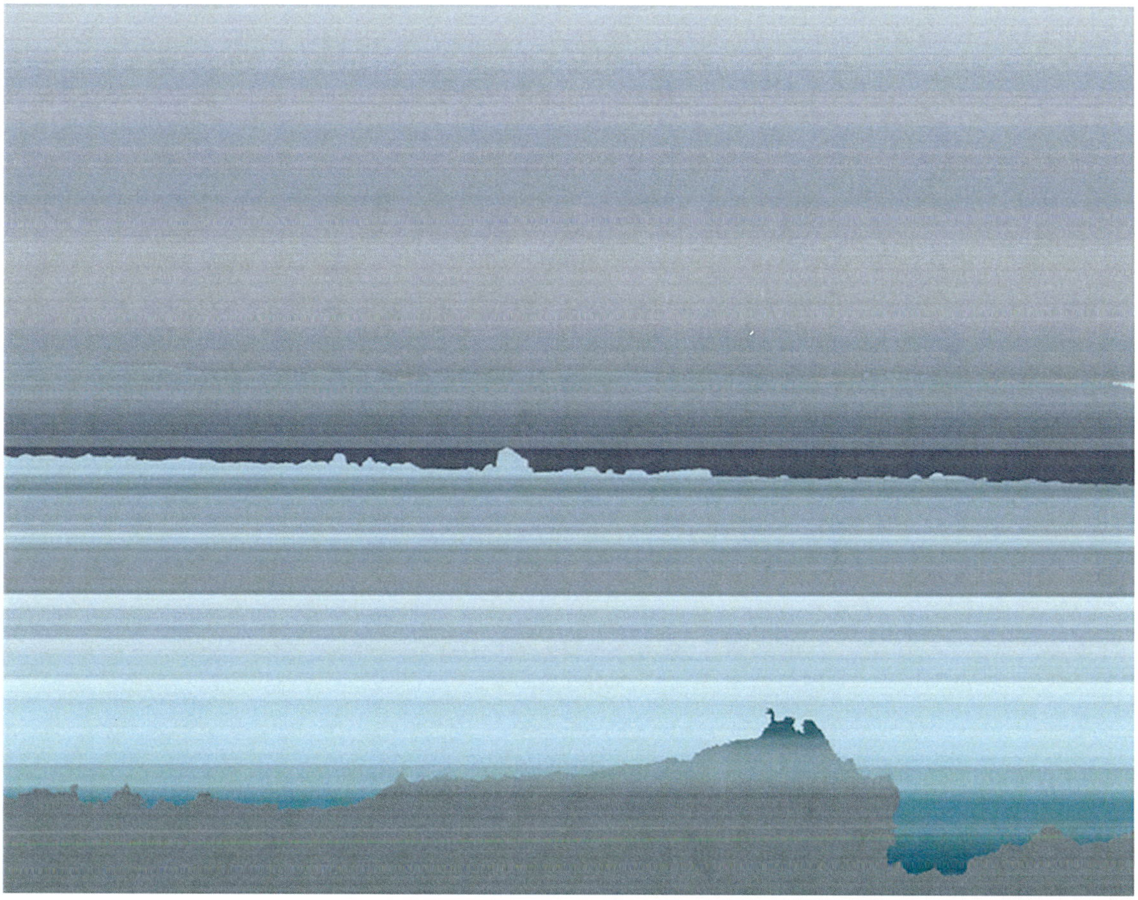

Daniel Ebenstein

Washington Square

Winter, 2014

Archival ink jet on
Exhibition Fiber paper

14 in x 20 in

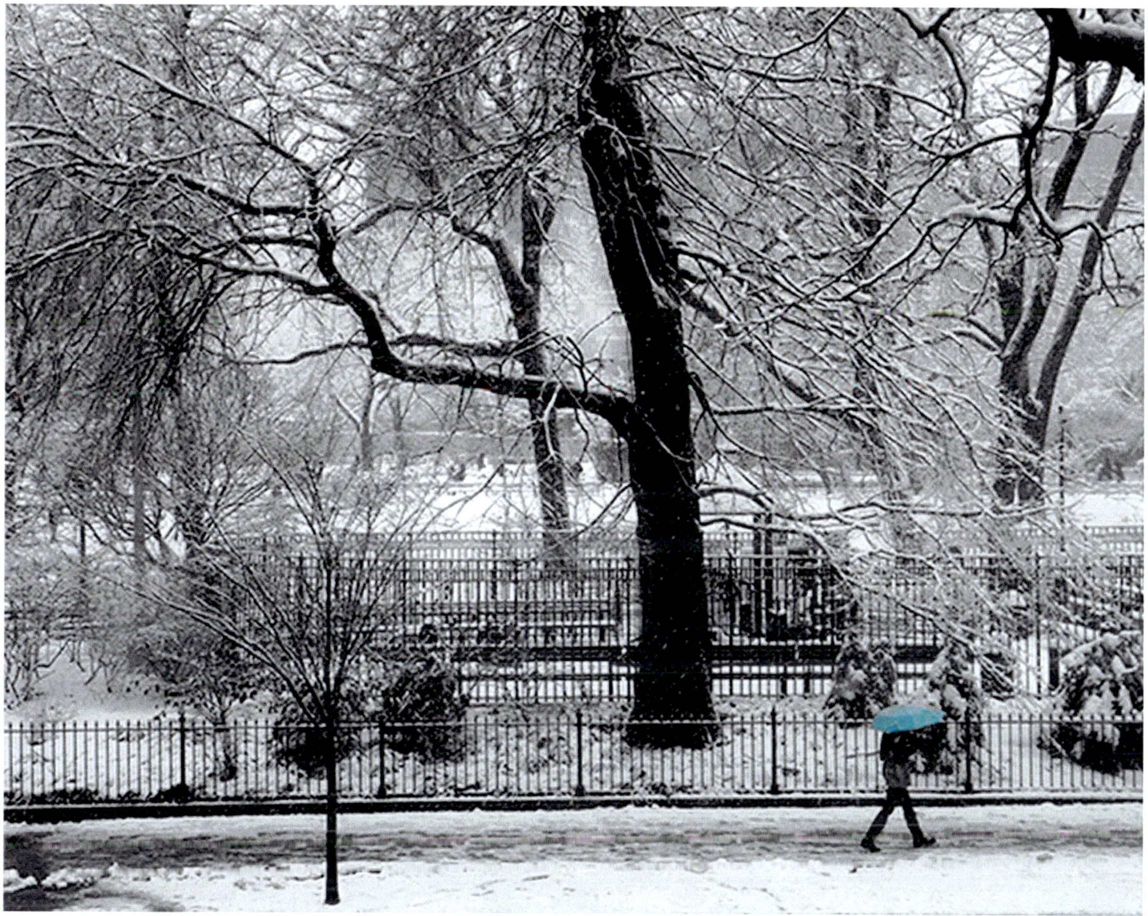

Winter Sunset
By Heather Stivison

Blinding bright winter sunlight
pierces through
tangled black skeletons of trees
painting shadows
of long gnarled fingers,
caressing
the swollen hillside,
and kissing
glistening snow
blushing scarlet
at its lover's
tender goodnight.

Susanah Howland

Snowing, 2015

Oil on Cardboard

12 in x 9 in

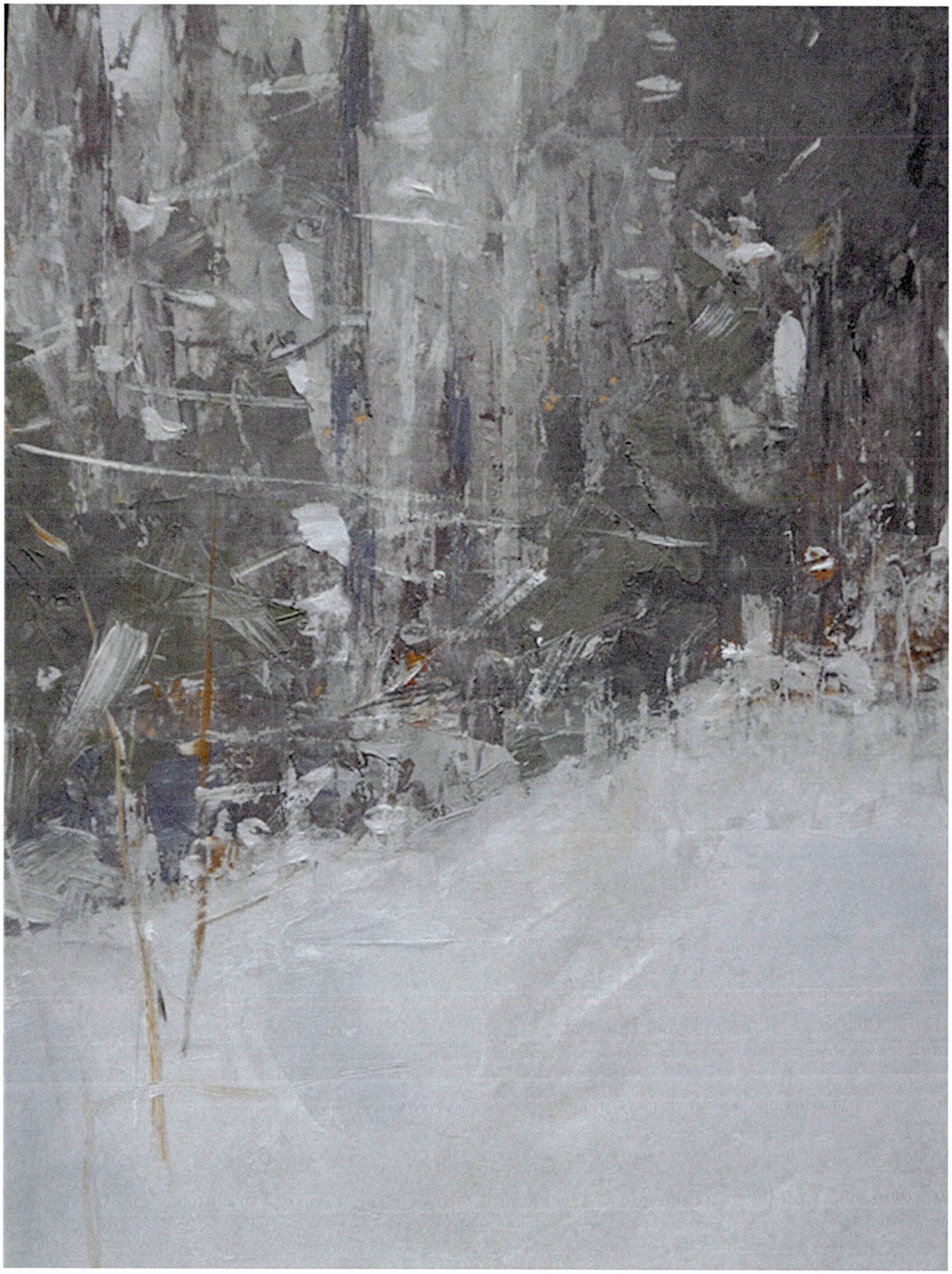

Susanah Howland

Wood's Edge, 2015

Oil on Cardboard

12 in x 9 in

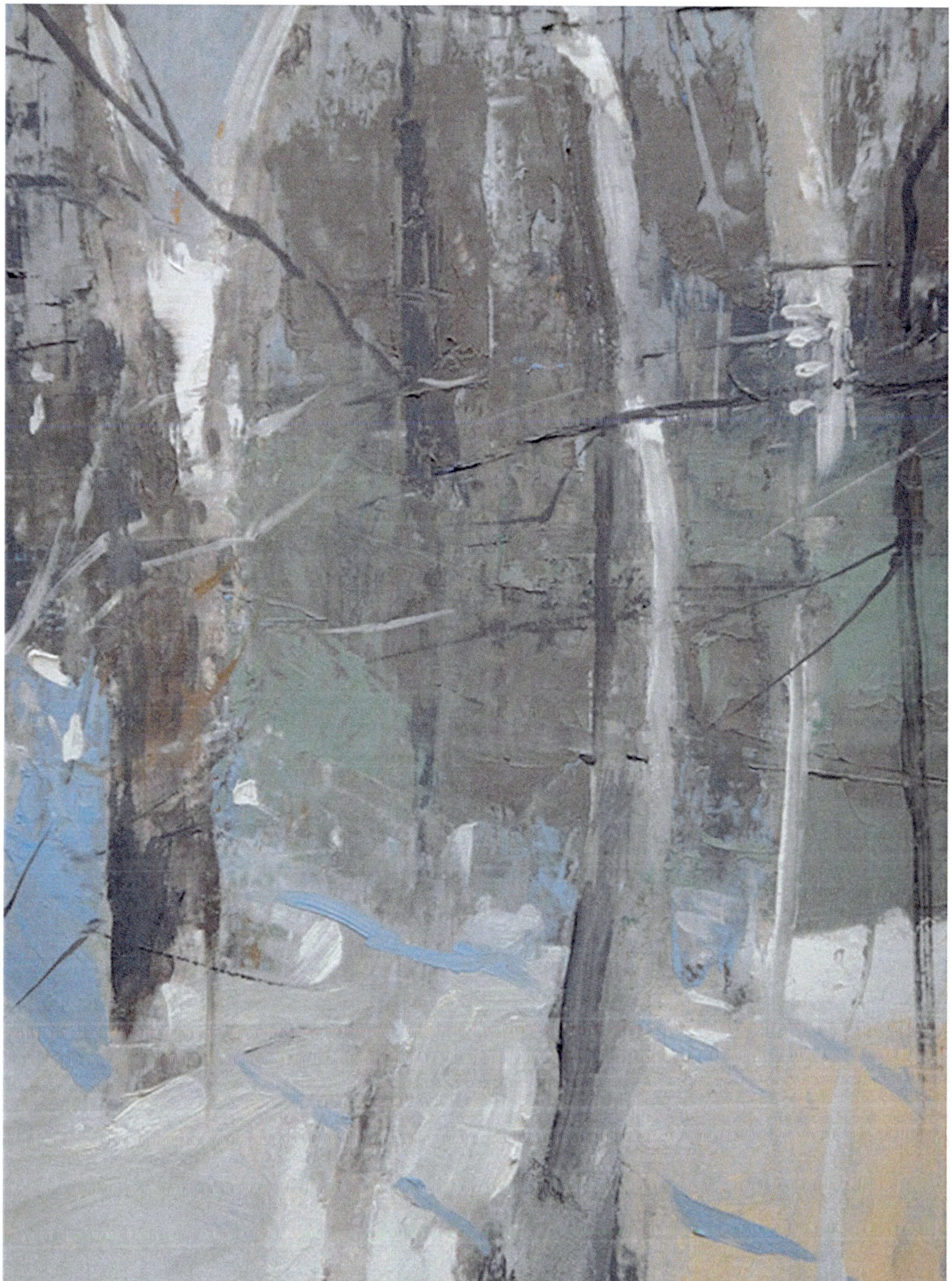

Susanah Howland

Winter, 2015

Oil on Cardboard

14 in x 12 in

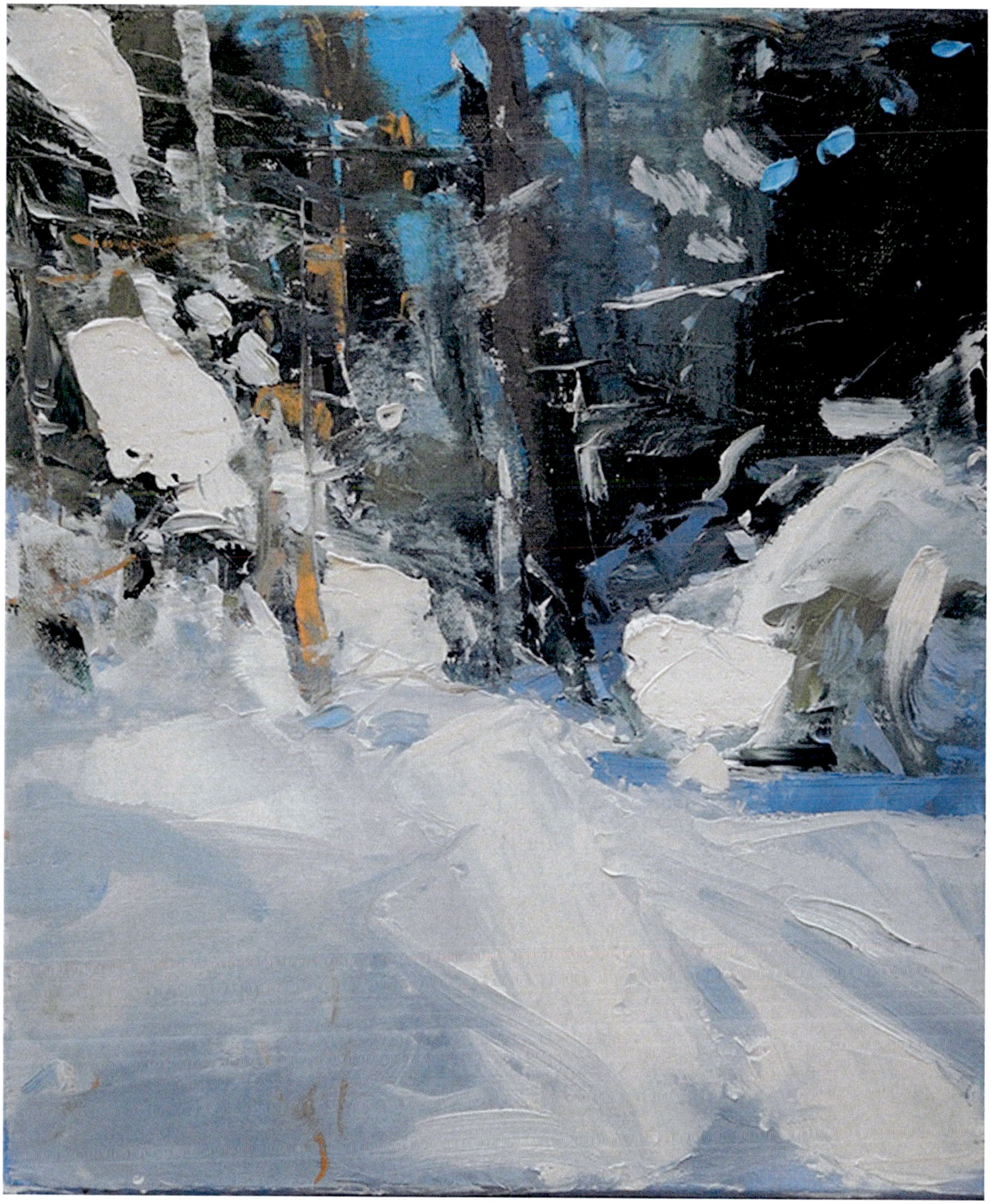

Susanah Howland

Snowy Field, 2015

Oil on Cardboard

9 in x 12 in

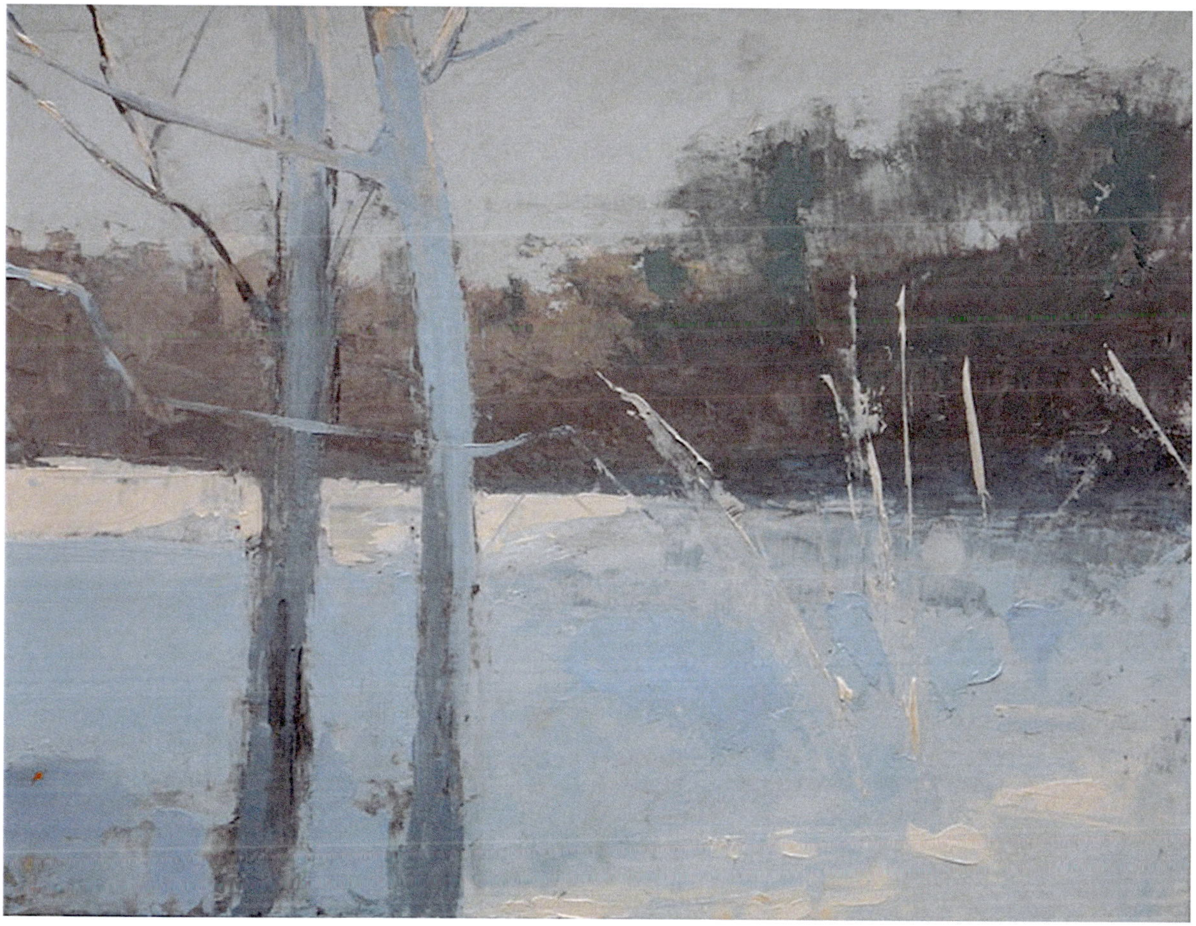

Ice Storm

By Kathryn Troxler

1

Dawn in the Snow Queen's realm –
cold white, reflected light
muted forms
encased in ice

In my glazed garden
myrtles bow to earth
swollen leaves,
flowers, mauve and frozen
topple the camellias

Jeweled plants – carnelian, jade –
grass magnified in crystal scabbards
entombed against
the forest's tracery

2

Light blazes through
this crystalline world
as the rising sun repeats itself
in myriad suns on every bough

The forest gleams with light
and rings with sound
mad tinkling of melting drops
cascading ice loads crashing down

3

Ice bonds released —
branches spring up
while tangled trees —-rent and broken —
begin their long subsidence into earth

Zintis Buzermanis

In Situ

Photograph

17 in x 12 in

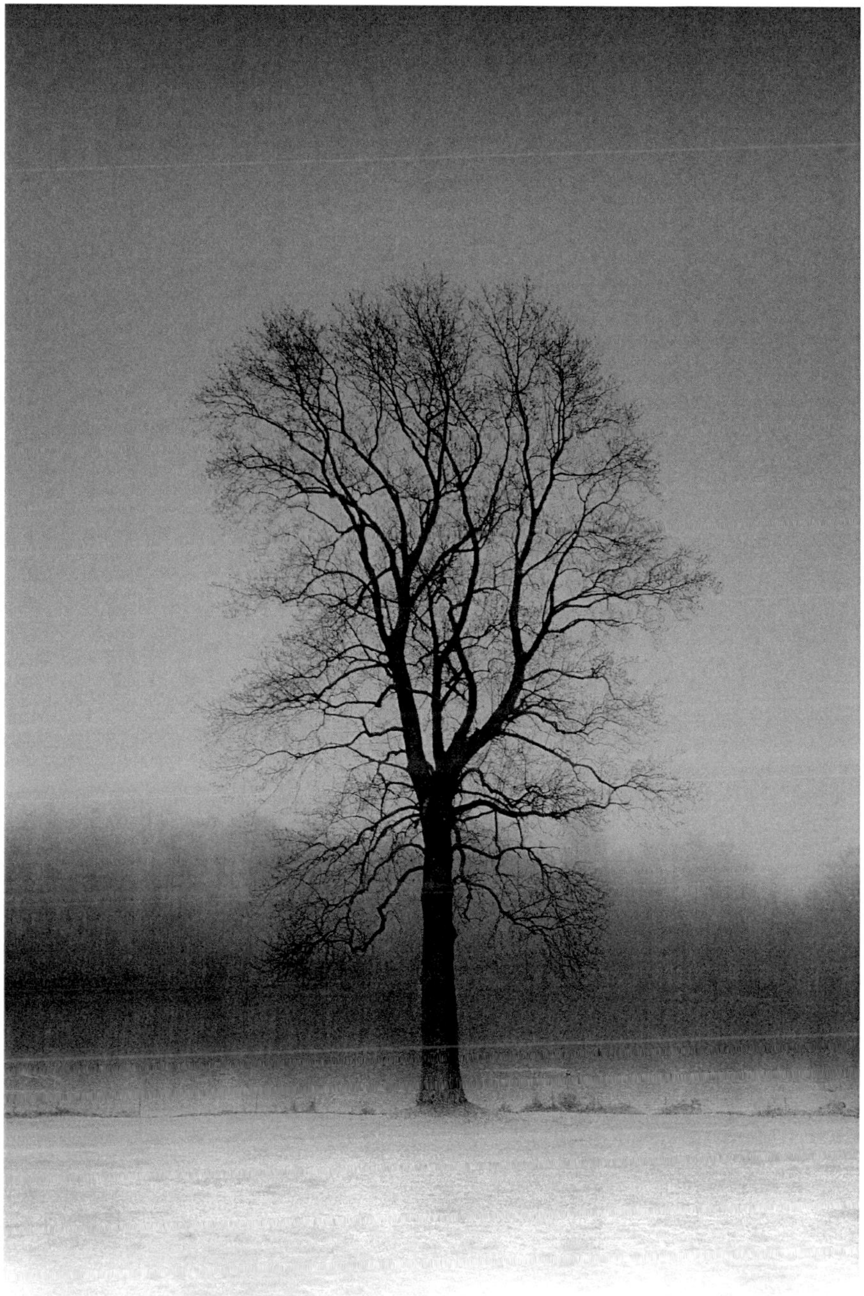

Zintis Buzermanis

In Situ II

Photograph

17 in x 12 in

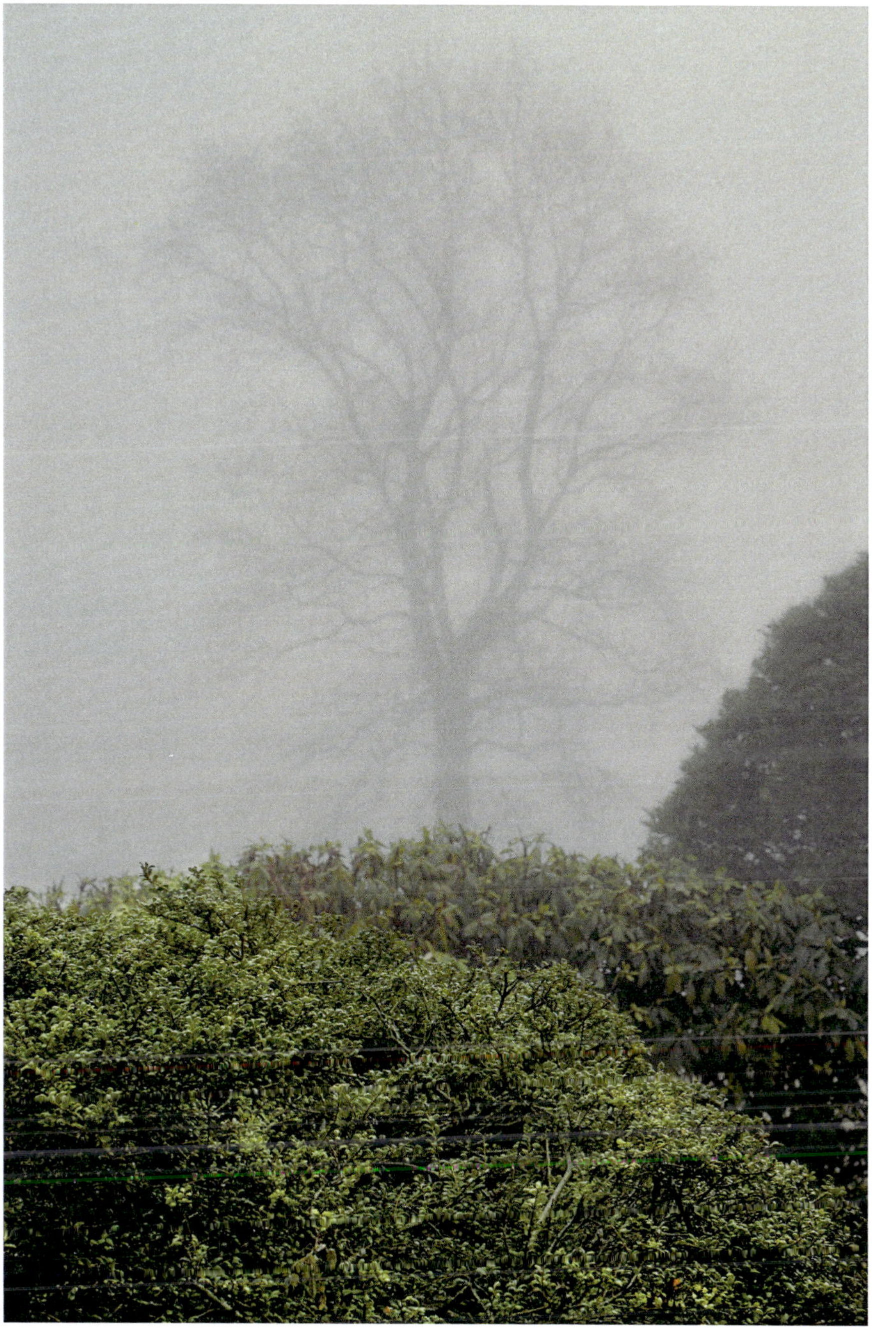

Zintis Buzermanis

Conifers at Dusk

Photograph

17 in x 12 in

Zintis Buzermanis

Snowstorm

Photograph

6 in x 9 in

Lake Brandt: Midwinter

By Kathryn Troxler

1

Walking north
along the frozen lake
on the distant shore
crystalline air makes visible
the fine tracery of trees
their budded branches
lined with snow —
radiant
in the light.

It seems I could reach out across the lake
through time and space suspended
and touch each one.

Today no moisture blurs
softens, blends
obscures or diminishes them —
their dazzling multiplicity
almost too much to bear

2

Sound

like a primeval serpent horn
or mighty conch

deep hollow resonance
plumbs the silence.

Vibrant crackling reverberates
through earth and air —

Song of the ice

A fine snaking line
scribes the surface.
Suddenly, unpredictably
where before it was not
this quick white snake
divides the lake
segments the frozen flow
the iced current patterns in sheeting layers
edges rippled.

At the inlet
a deep welling flow
winding toward spring
weakens the surface.
The moving current below
cracks the ice
and it begins to melt
in the sun.

3

Walking back
all is changed.
The ice —
tan in the inlet—
casts an orange glow.
Coral beech leaves fill the woods
Quick crunching footsteps mark the snow

I'm on my way home —
logos quickening my heart.

Joyce Chen

Twigs

Acrylic and Oil on Canvas

20 in x 16 in

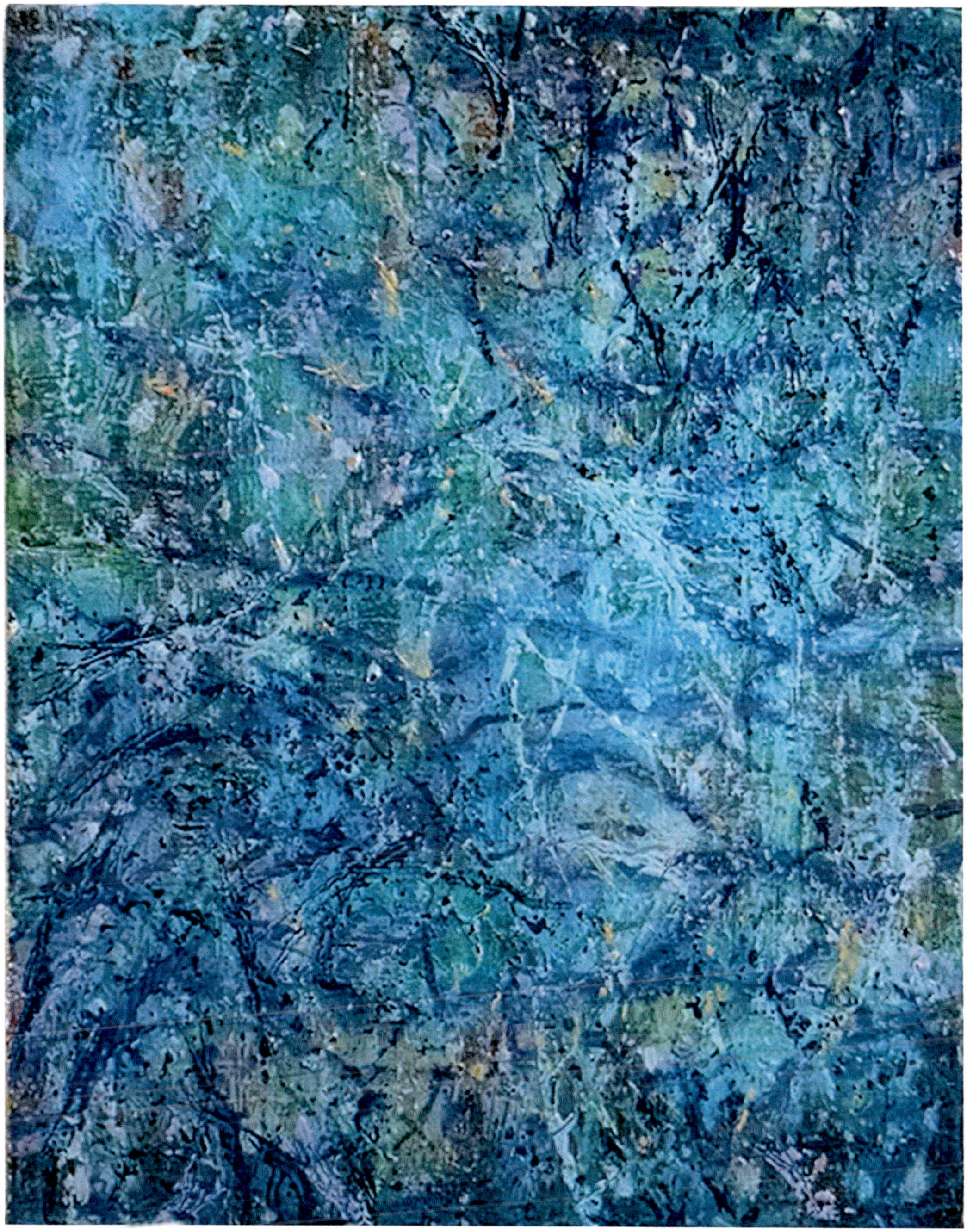

Mariella Bisson

Stowe, The First Snow

Mixed Media on Linen

50 in x 38 in

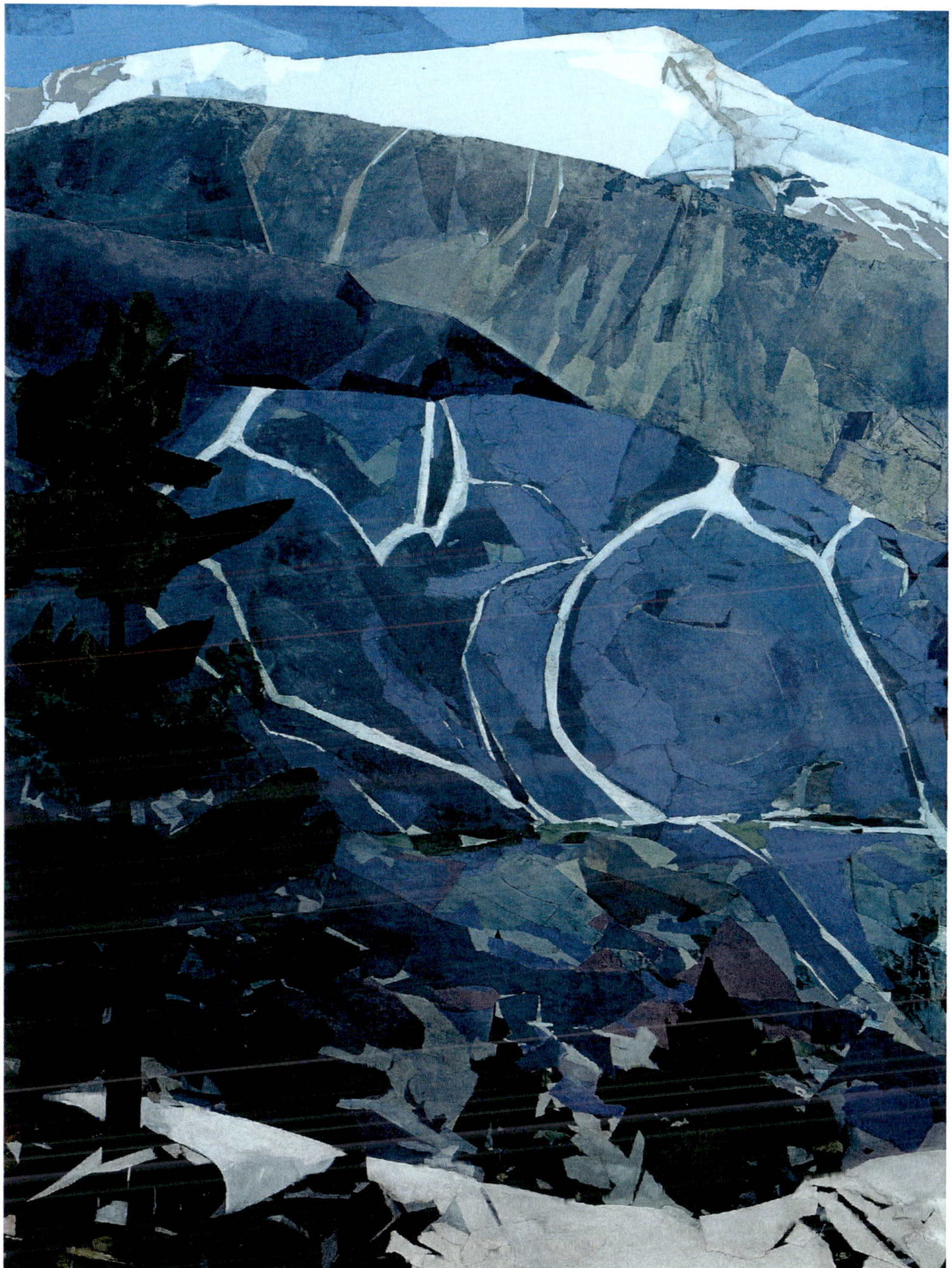

Mariella Bisson

Breckenridge, Twilight, Ski Trails*, *2007

Gouache painting on paper

19 in x 25 in

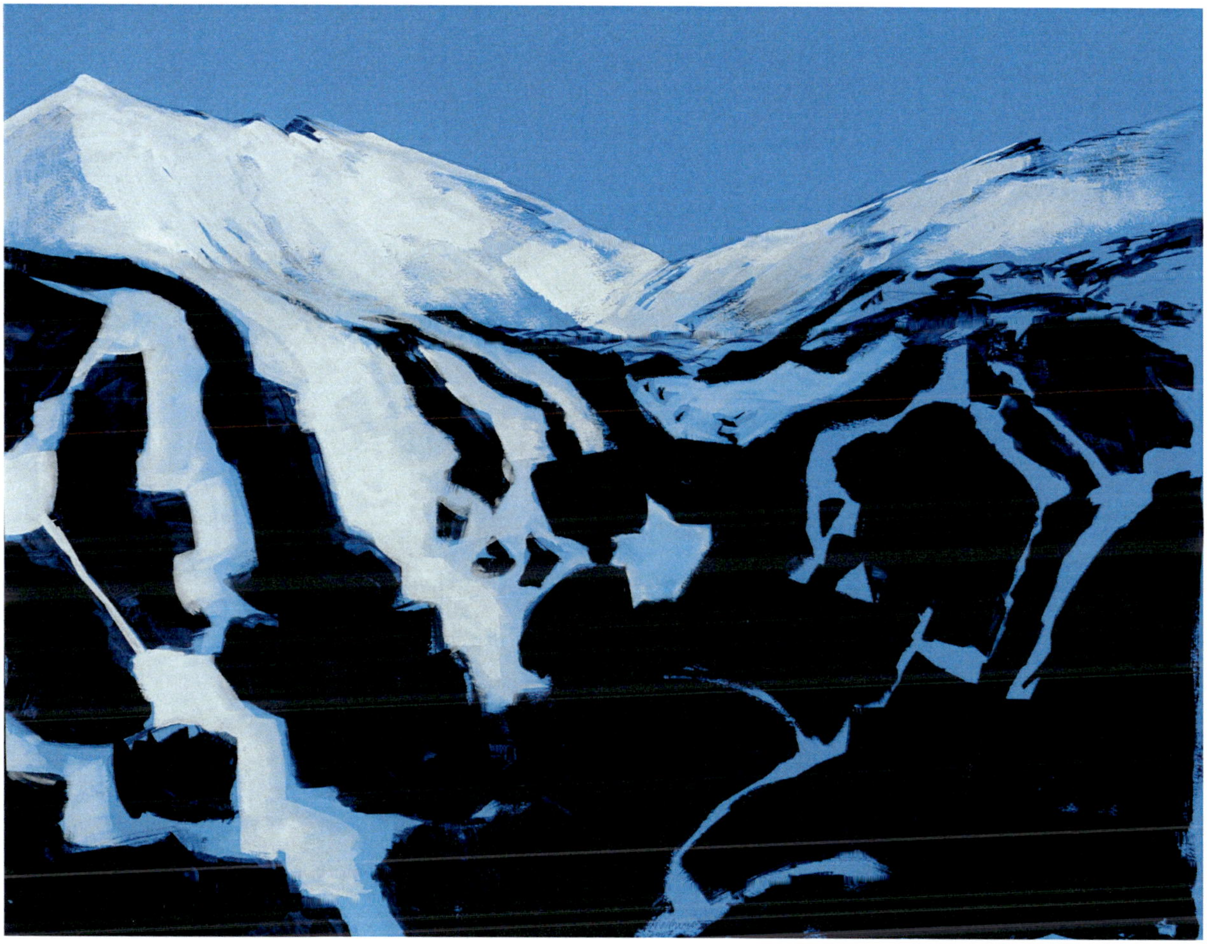

Elizabeth Braun

Ice (Stained Glass 3)

Digital Photograph

16 in x 20 in

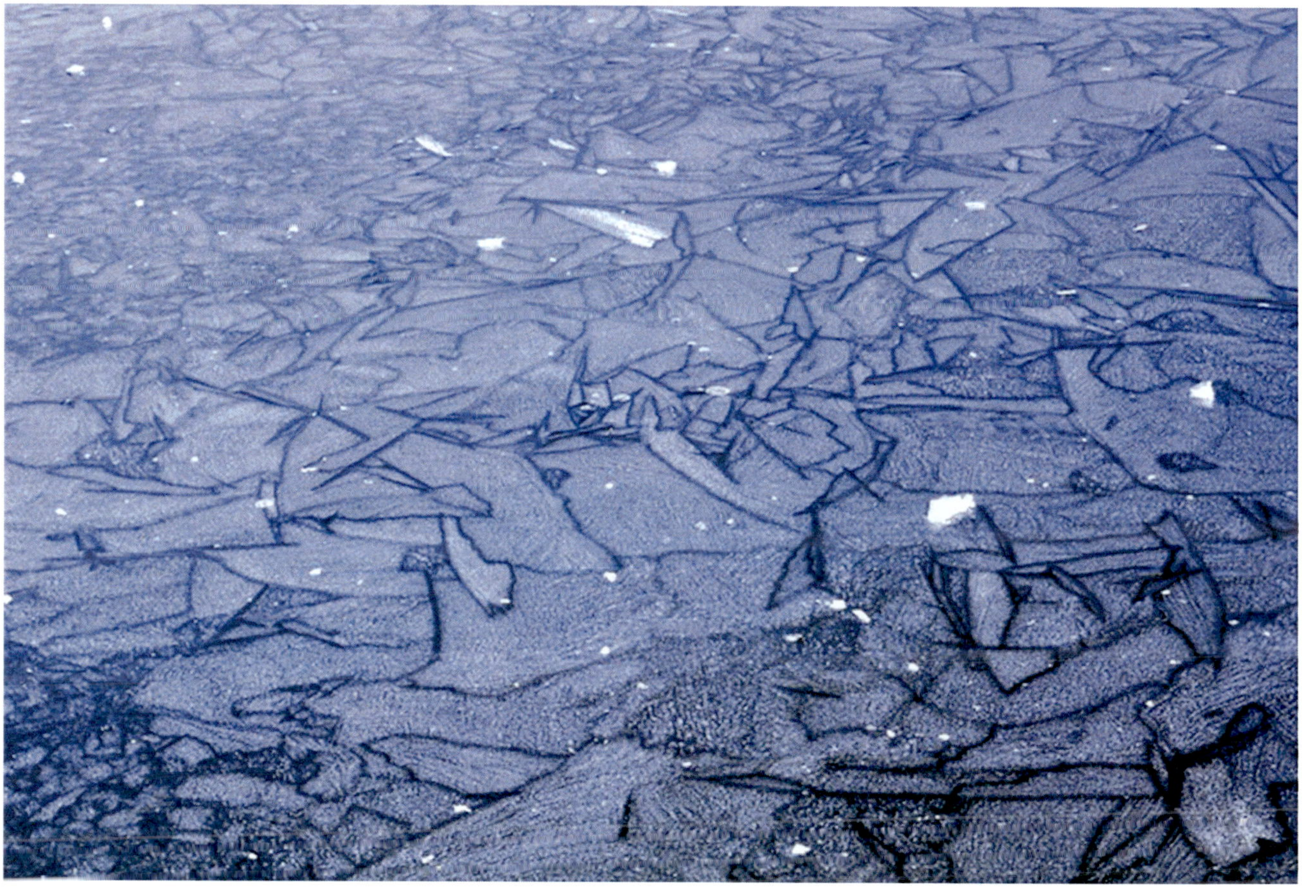

Elizabeth Braun

Ice (Bubbles}

Digital Photograph

20 in x 16 in

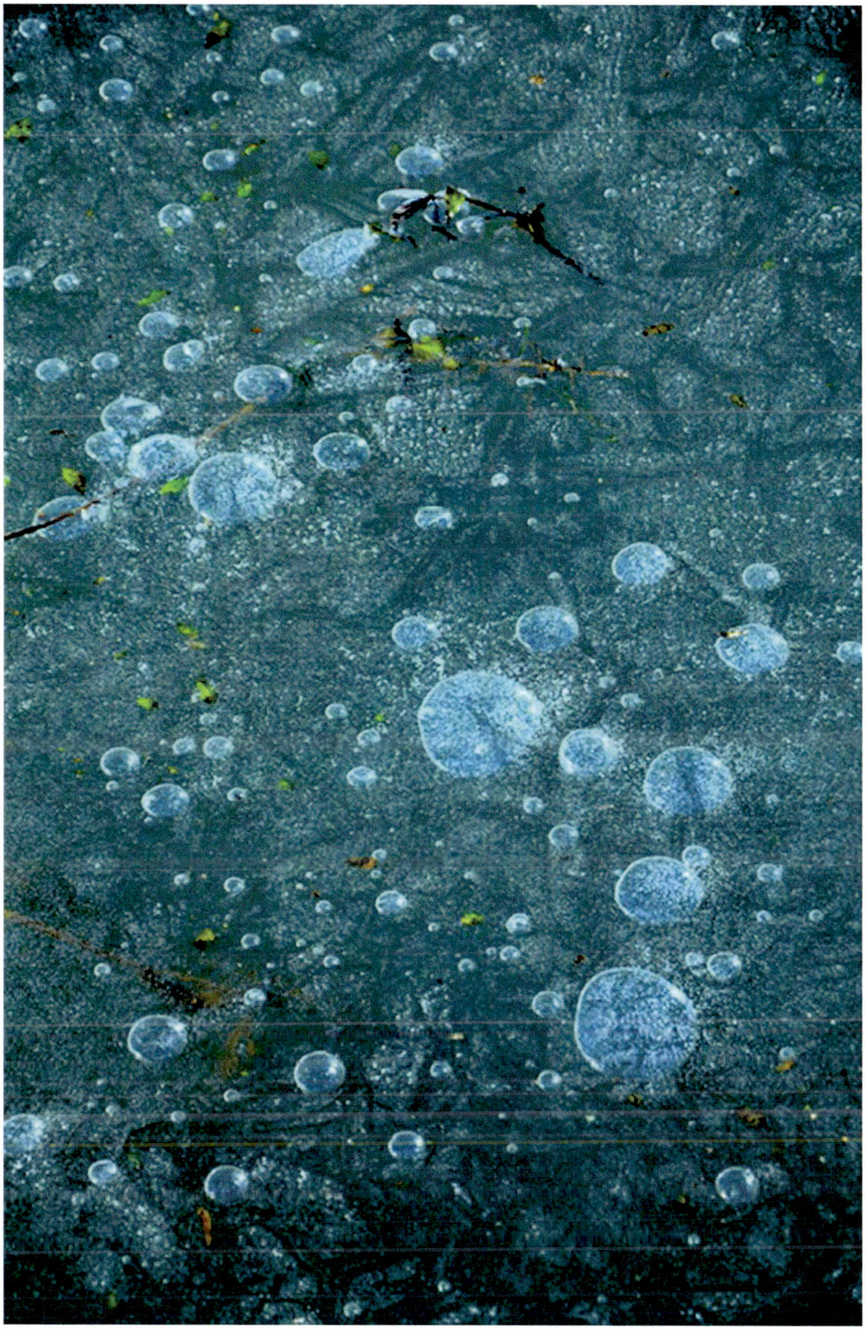

Elizabeth Braun

Geometry

Digital Photograph

12 in x 18 in

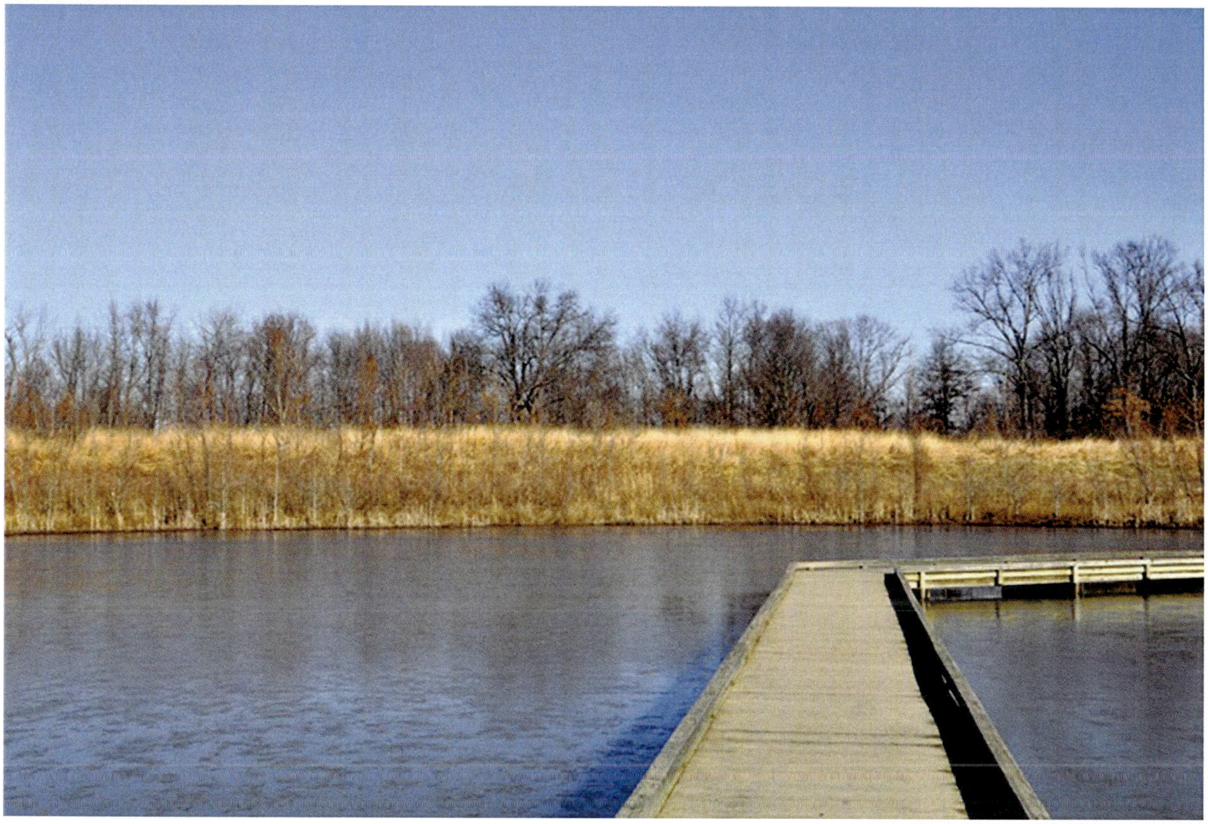

Elizabeth Braun

Winter Berries

Digital Photograph

8 in x 10 in

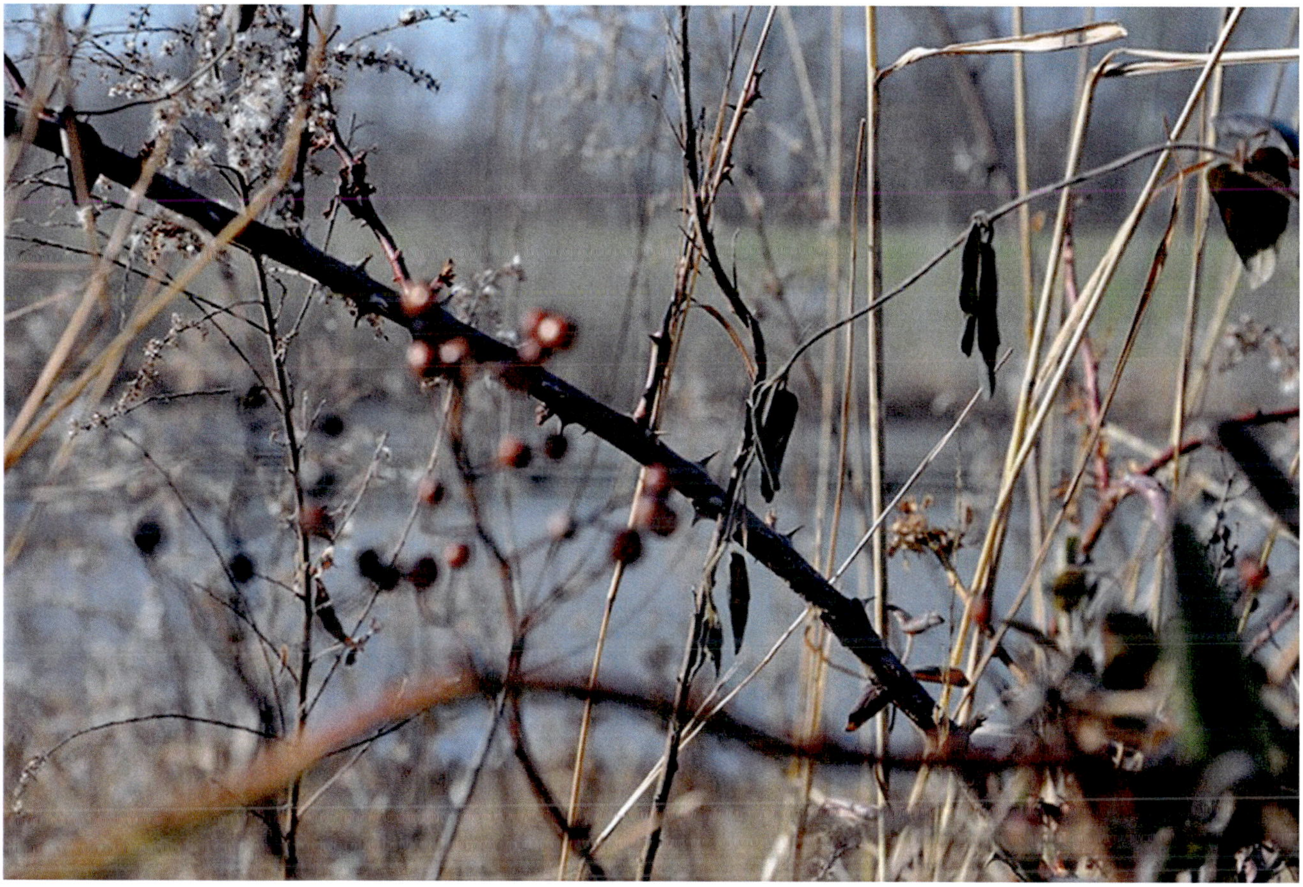

Graehound

Dark Chatter

Mixed Water Media

12 in x 10 in

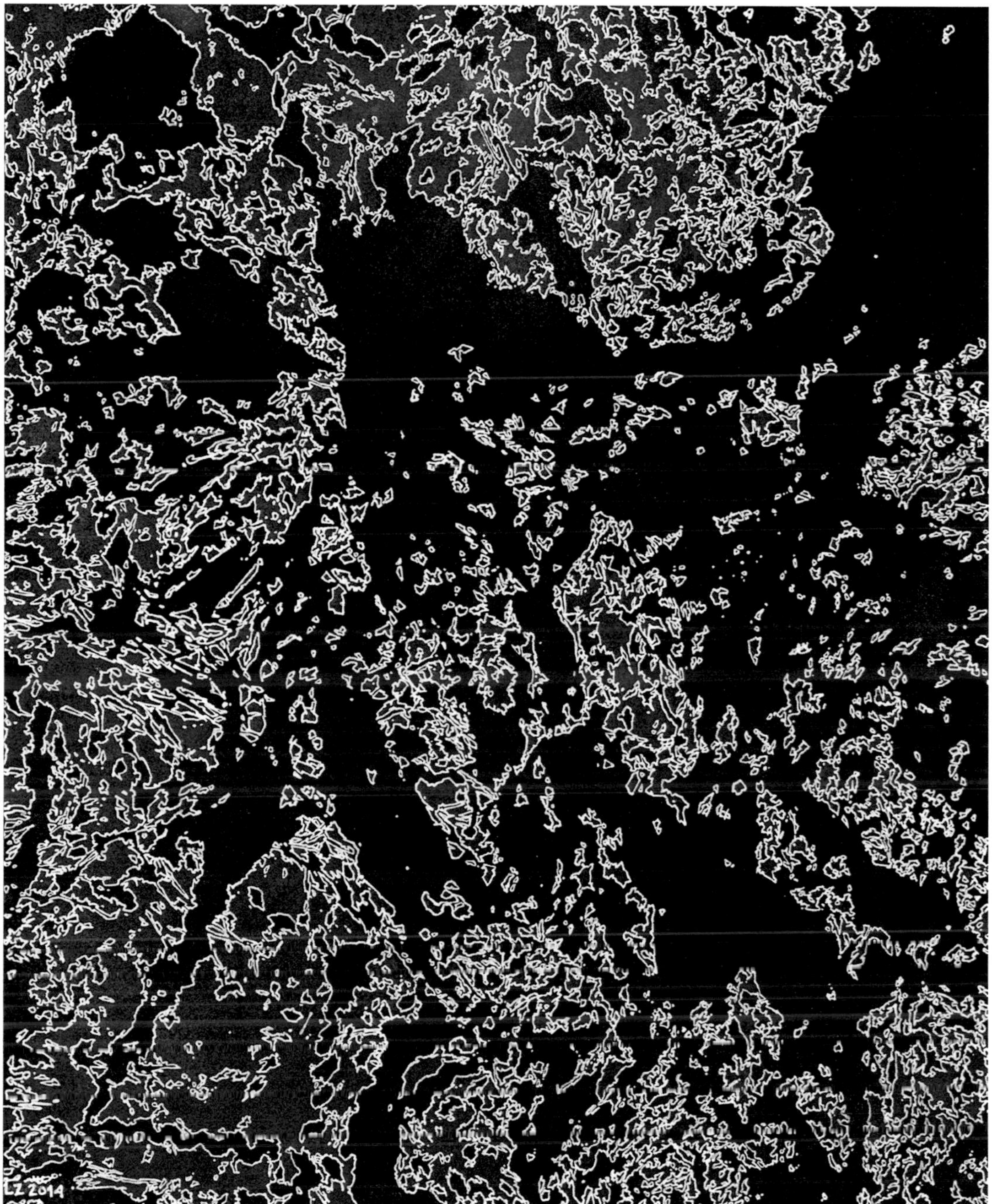
LZ 2014

Kiva

By Kathryn Troxler

One by one
they descend
into the kiva
and circle the fire pit
shaking bone rattles
beating drums
they chant through the night.

Bodies gleam and darken
in flickering light—
their looming shadows interwoven
with gods and ancestors
in a moving pattern —
they merge
in smoky tribal space.

The womblike room pulses
with sound and movement
as past, present and future
converge.
Once again they dance
the circle of the year
into being.

At dawn
one by one
they climb their ladder
to the stars
out
into the crisp
cold air.

Lynn Simarski

Losing Ground/Courtney's

Digital Photograph

7 in x 13 in

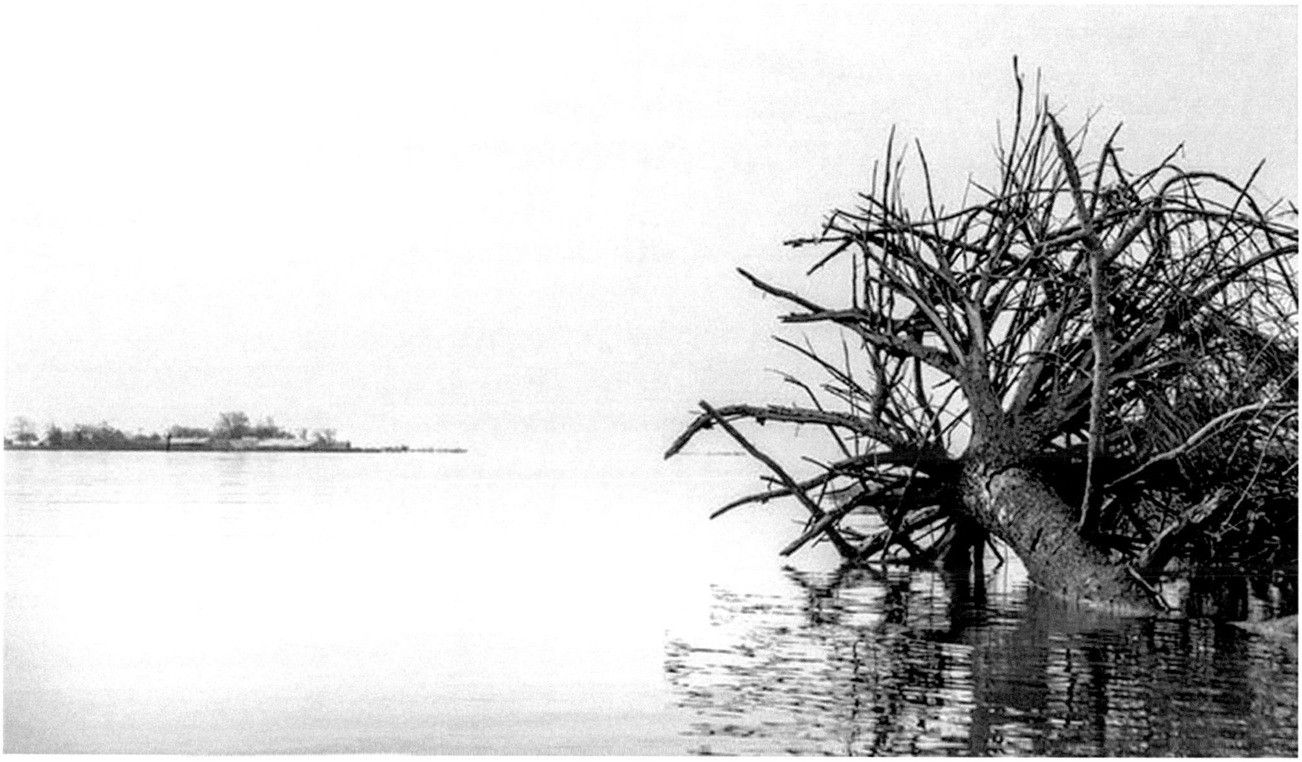

Lynn Simarski

Secret Orchard

Digital Photograph

8 in x 18 in

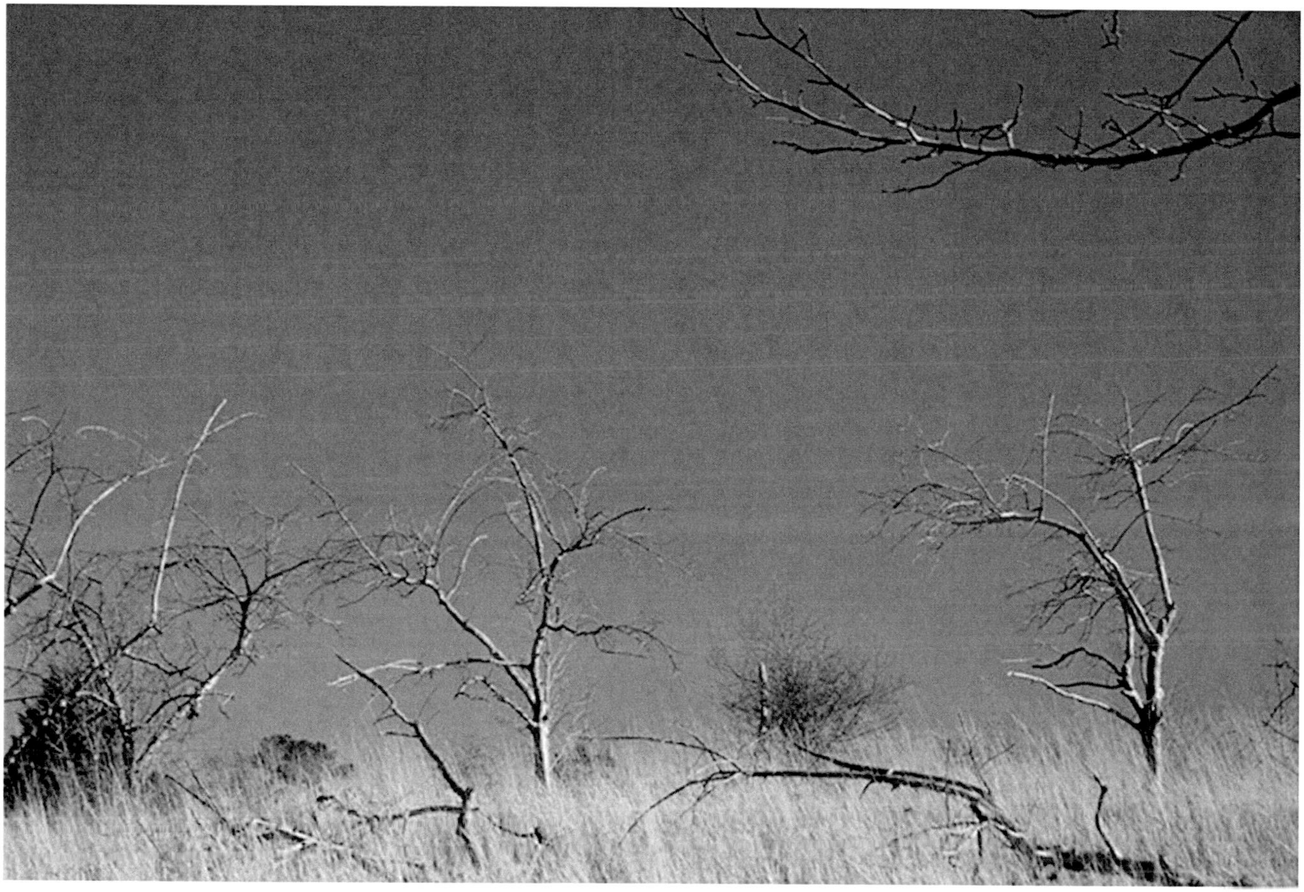

Lynn Simarski

Abacus

Digital Photograph

13 in x 19 in

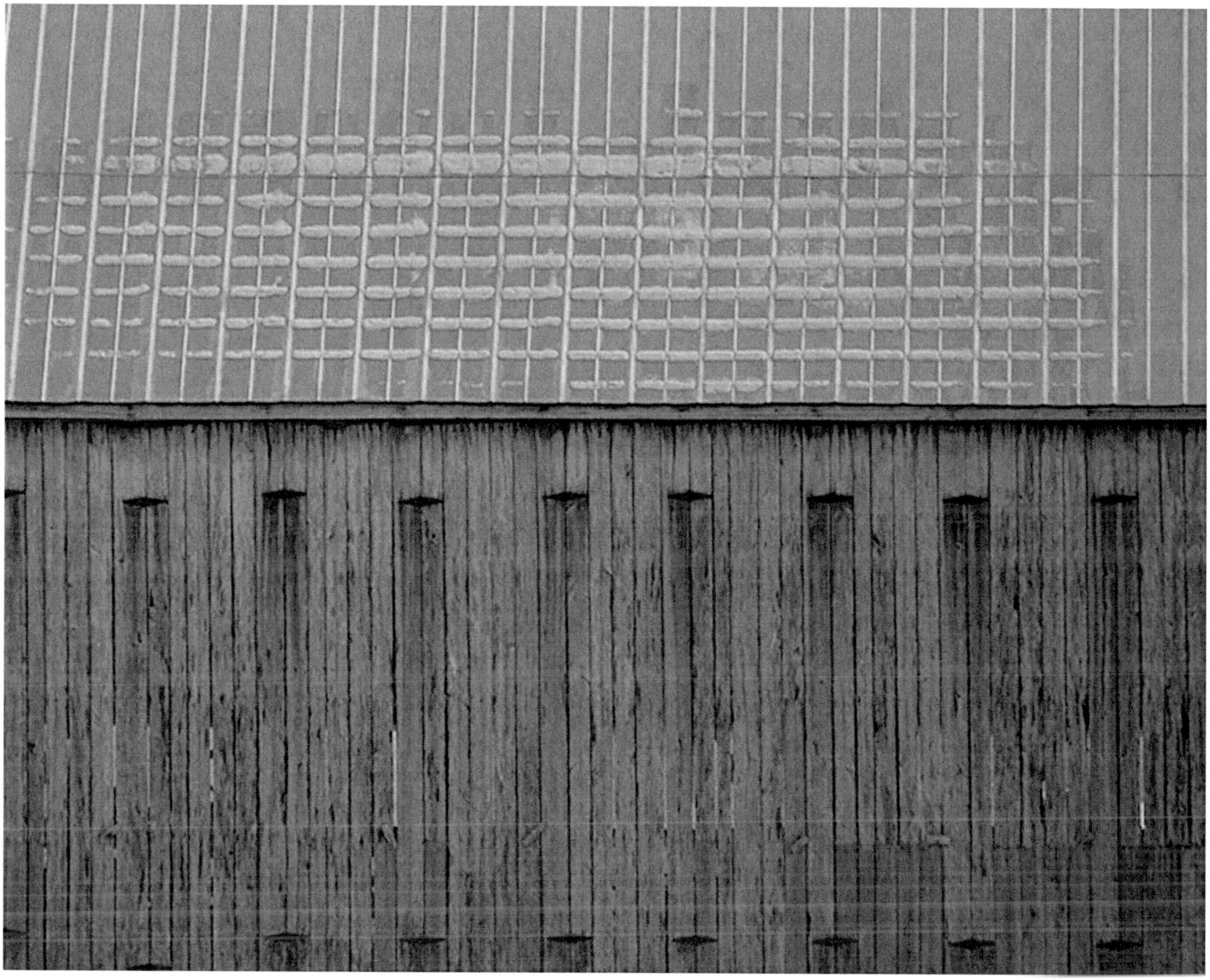

In November

By Kathryn Troxler

Can I
like a Chinese sage
internalize this autumn day
distill from muted light and palette
evanescence and enduring form
to sustain me through the days to come?

The woods disheveled
presage winter
Stark trees
skeletal and strong
gold apricot and russet leaves
staccato brilliance on dark ground.

My driveway
wet from last night's rain
gives back translucent leaf forms
impressed like memories upon it
while fresh leaves
scatter down

As the season
gathers to itself
the last remains of summer
it brings to me beauty's harvest
sustenance
for a winter bound soul.

Kerfe Roig

23 Names For Snow

Paper Collage

9 in x 13 in

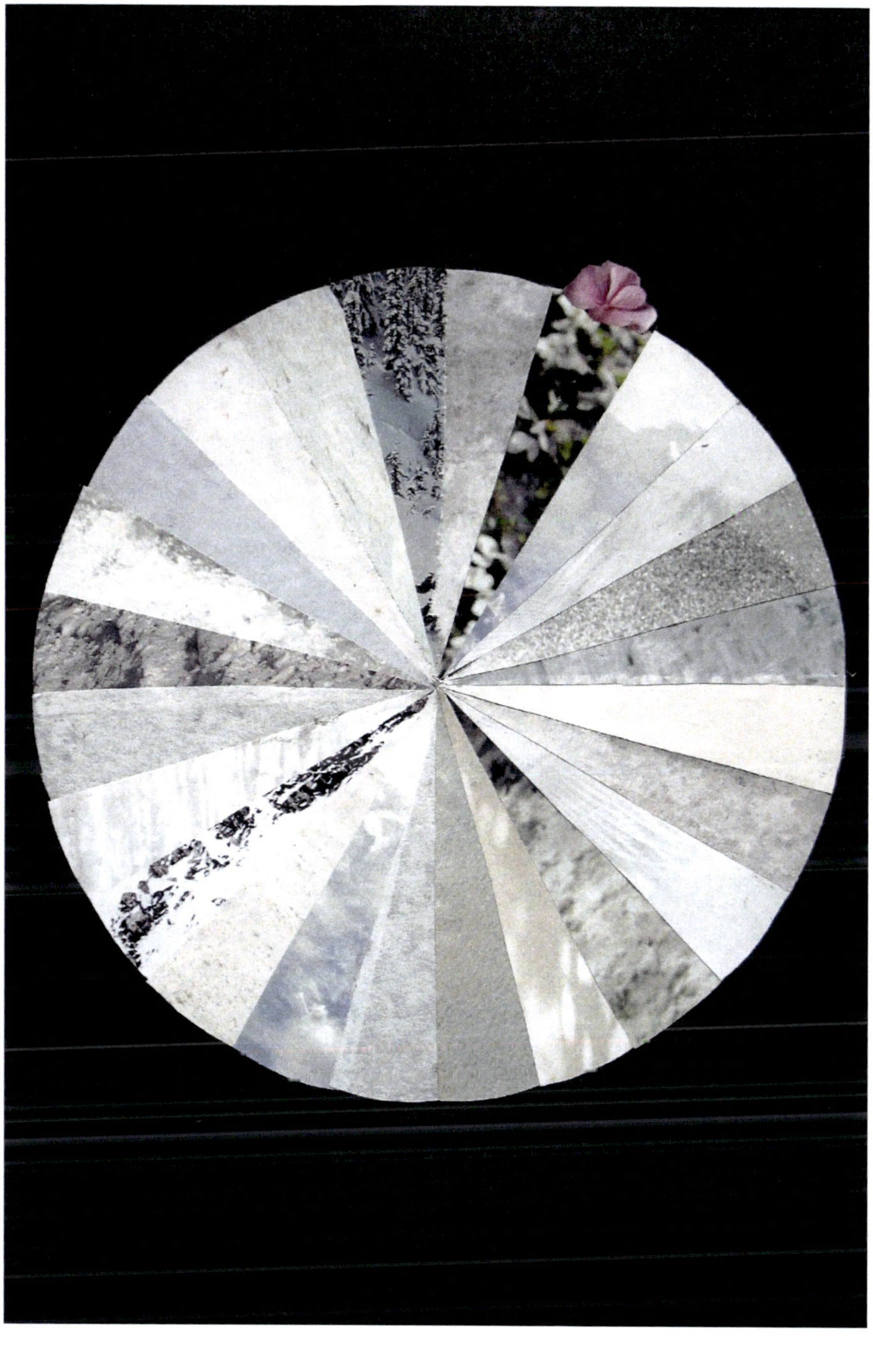

Kerfe Roig

There's A Crow Flying 3

Monoprint with Collage and Embroidery

18 in x 9 in

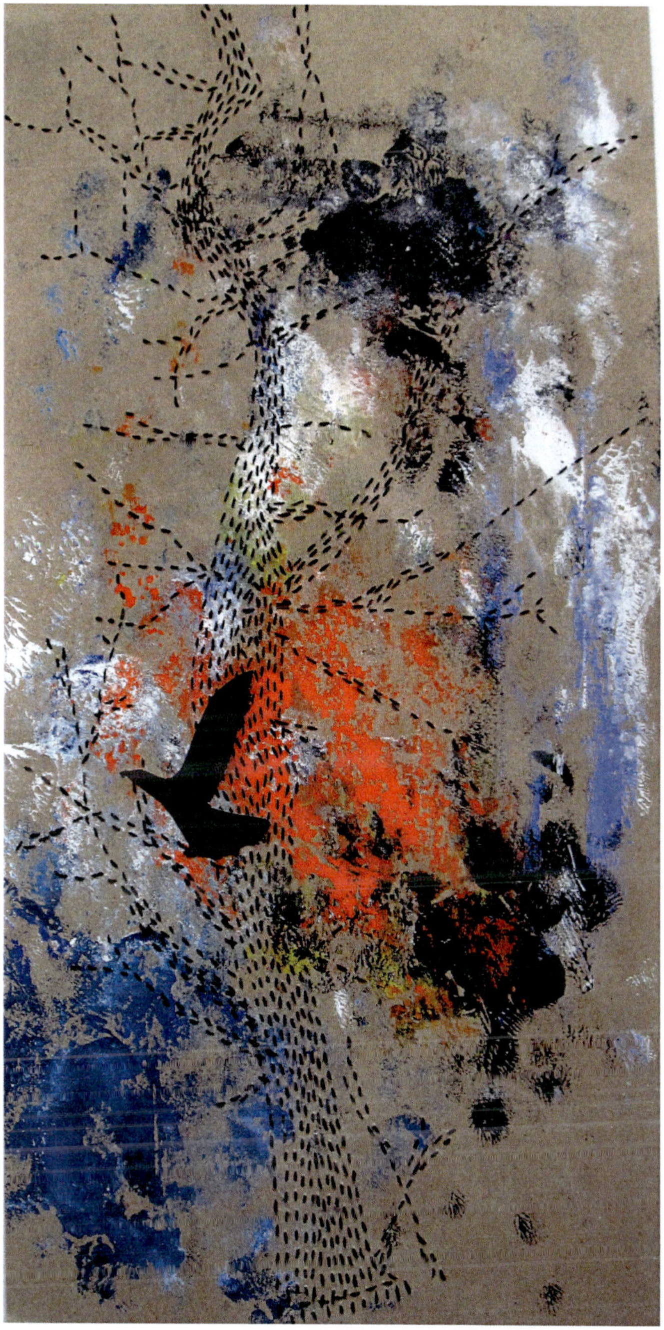

Clare Olivares

Dark Lines

Mixed Media

7 in x 4.5 in

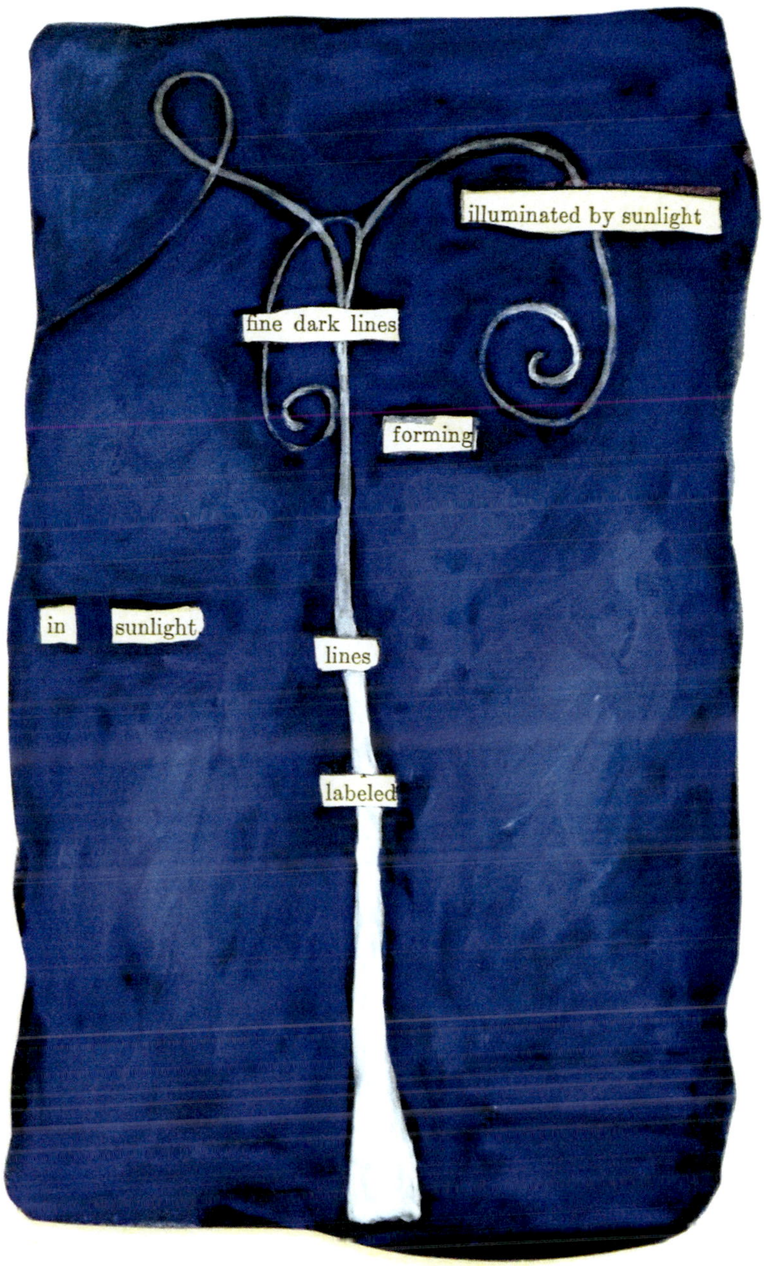
illuminated by sunlight
fine dark lines
forming
in
sunlight
lines
labeled

Clare Olivares

Air in the Room

Mixed Media

7 in x 4.5 in

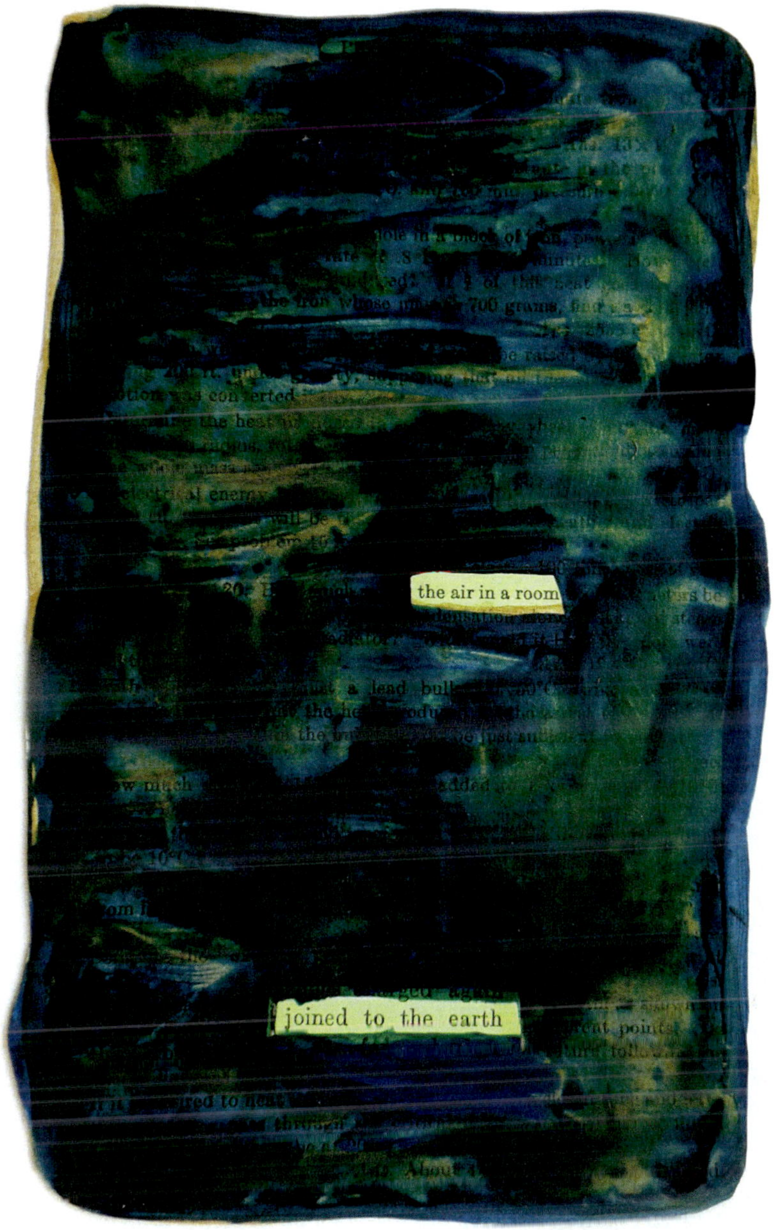
the air in a room
joined to the earth

The Longest Night

By Bridget Robertson

The Longest Night...

I am a child of Winter.

Literally.

I was the second child in my family born on December 25.

My mother had years of traditions that placed Santa Claus on Christmas Eve and two birthday cakes with separate birthday presents on Christmas morning.

Yet, what I honor and love is the longest night of the year, the Blessed Winter Solstice

My time was spent at a grandmothers home tucked into a tiny town in the Wisconsin countryside

Resting on the shores of a beloved lake, usually semi frozen

Water in any form is my element.

We were far from artificial light that dims the night sky and stars from view. I could see them all on a clear night.

Cold with sometimes fallen snow, I simply was bundled to stay outside on this treasured night.

If cloudy, my love and awe were not dampened.

I have cherished this dark all of my life.

Others will celebrate a birth tonight,

I start that tomorrow, revering both Mother and child.

This is my tradition.

I claim it as only my own.

I light no candles.

No fires are burned.

Know this night on its own terms. It needs no illumination. That time will come soon enough.

If I must , I speak only in whispers.

Better to hear the silence.

No rush, no hurry, just being enveloped by that which is wrongly declared hostile.

This is my home.

Give me a north wind with many long winter nights.

I will relish them until I no longer exist.

For in this night, in this darkness, a hibernation of the senses,

I meet my soul from a time I have yet to know.

She is old, wearing life on her face,

always fierce, sometimes stark,

I love her deeply.

She can be found here, on this, the longest night.

Blessings to all,

Bridget Robertson

Diane Farr

Solitude

Oil on Canvas

12 in x 12 in

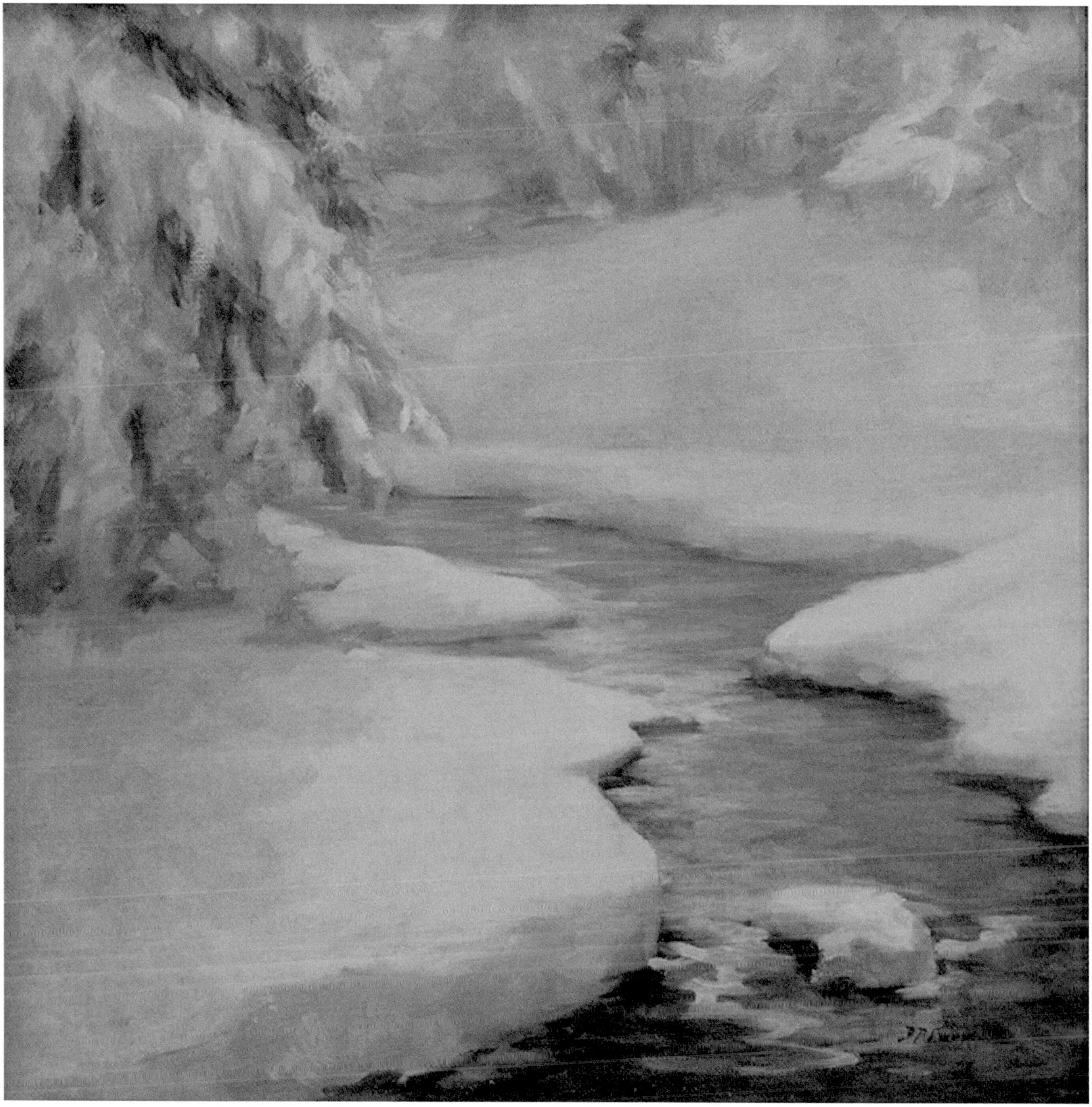

Diane Farr

Winter Field

Oil on Canvas

18 in x 24 in

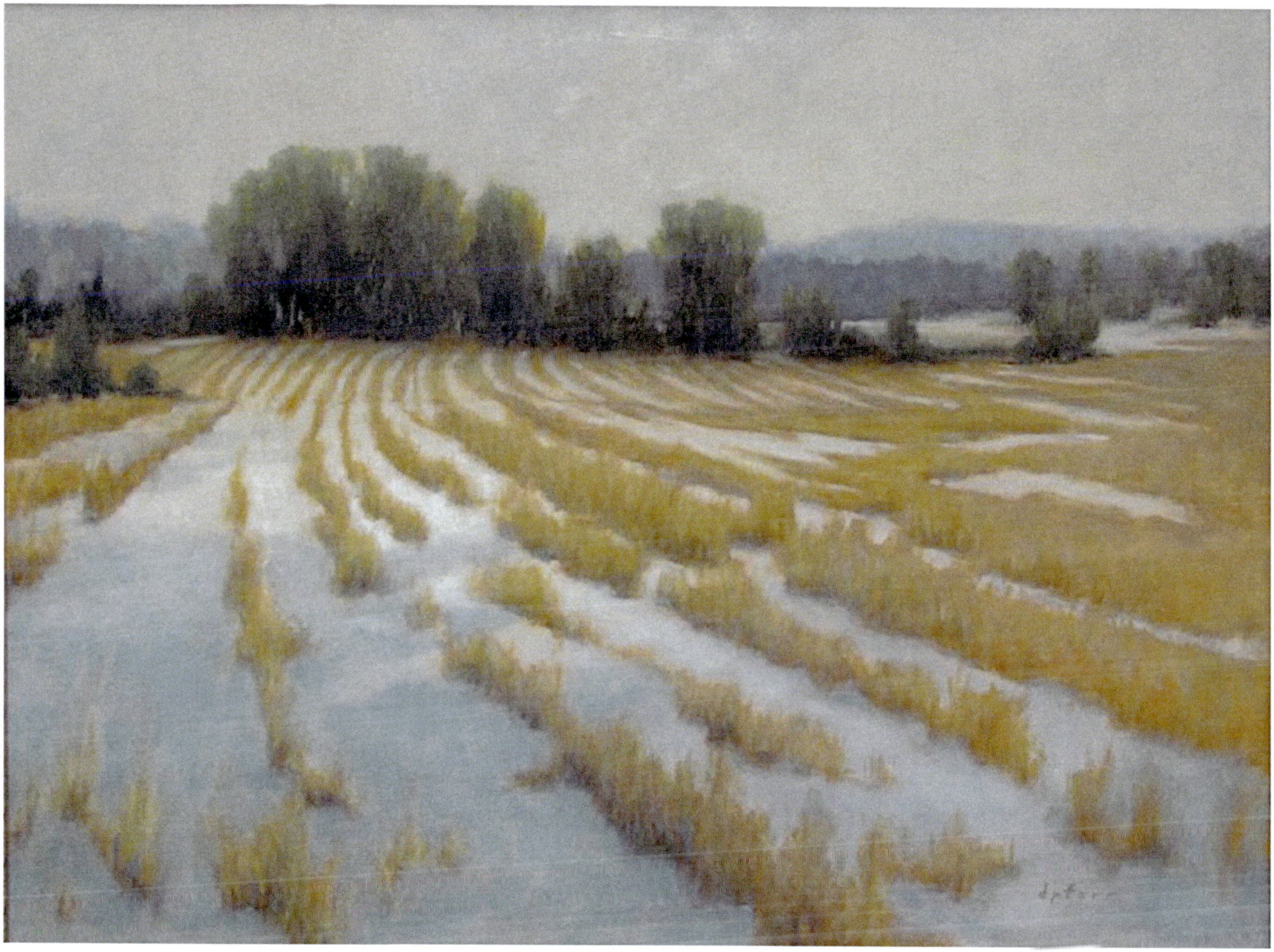

Lisa Nankivil

Skylight

Oil on Canvas

26 in x 42 in

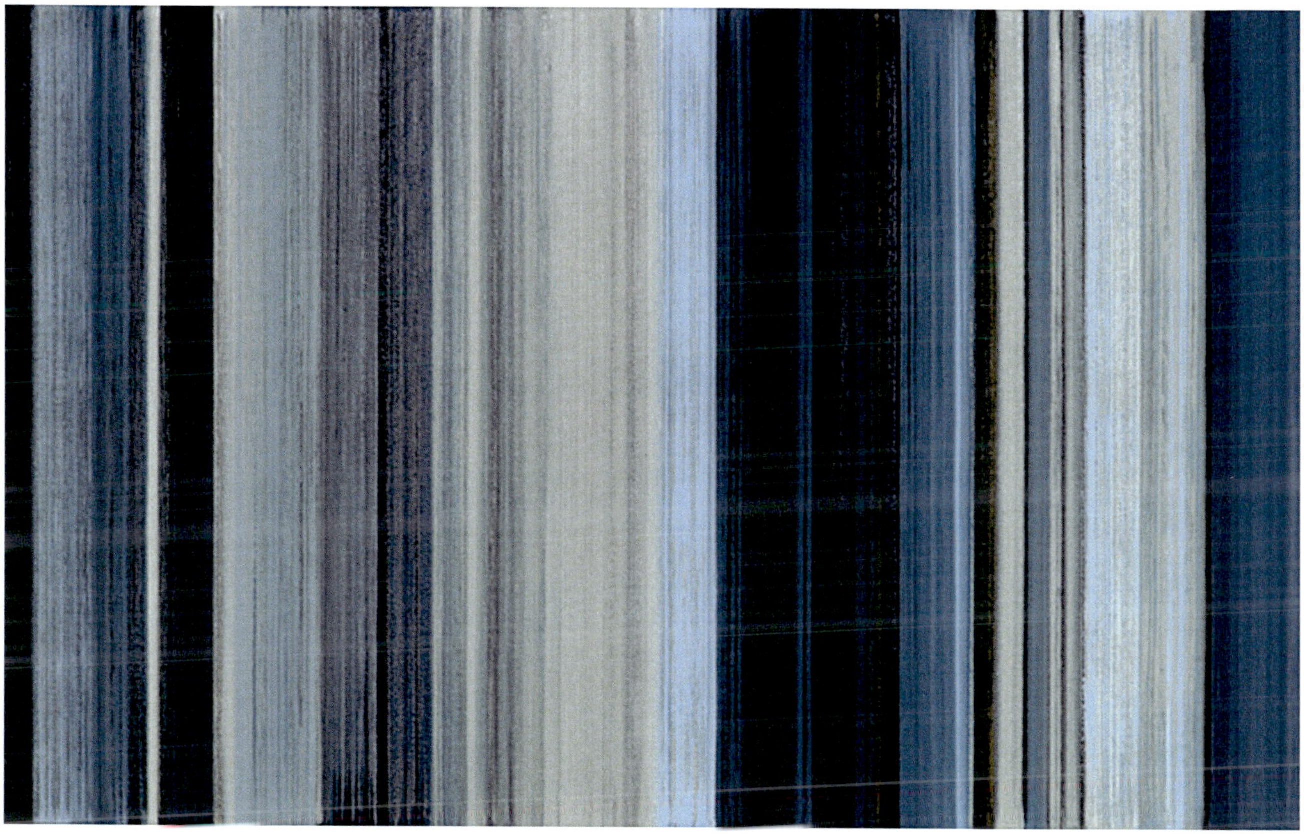

Lisa Nankivil

Hemisphere

Oil on Canvas

48 in x 54 in

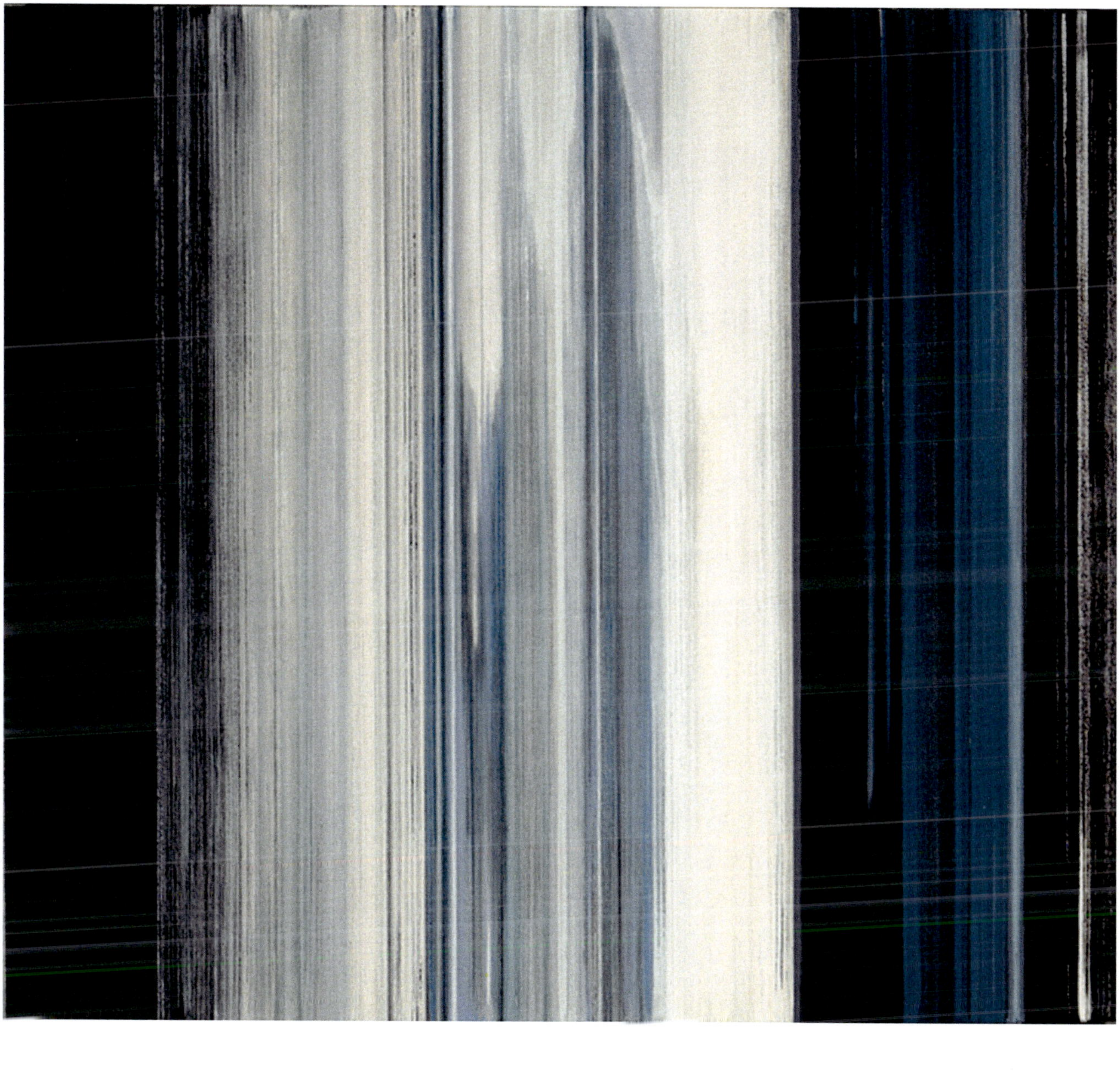

Lisa Nankivil

Immutable Dream

Oil on Canvas

40 in x 32 in

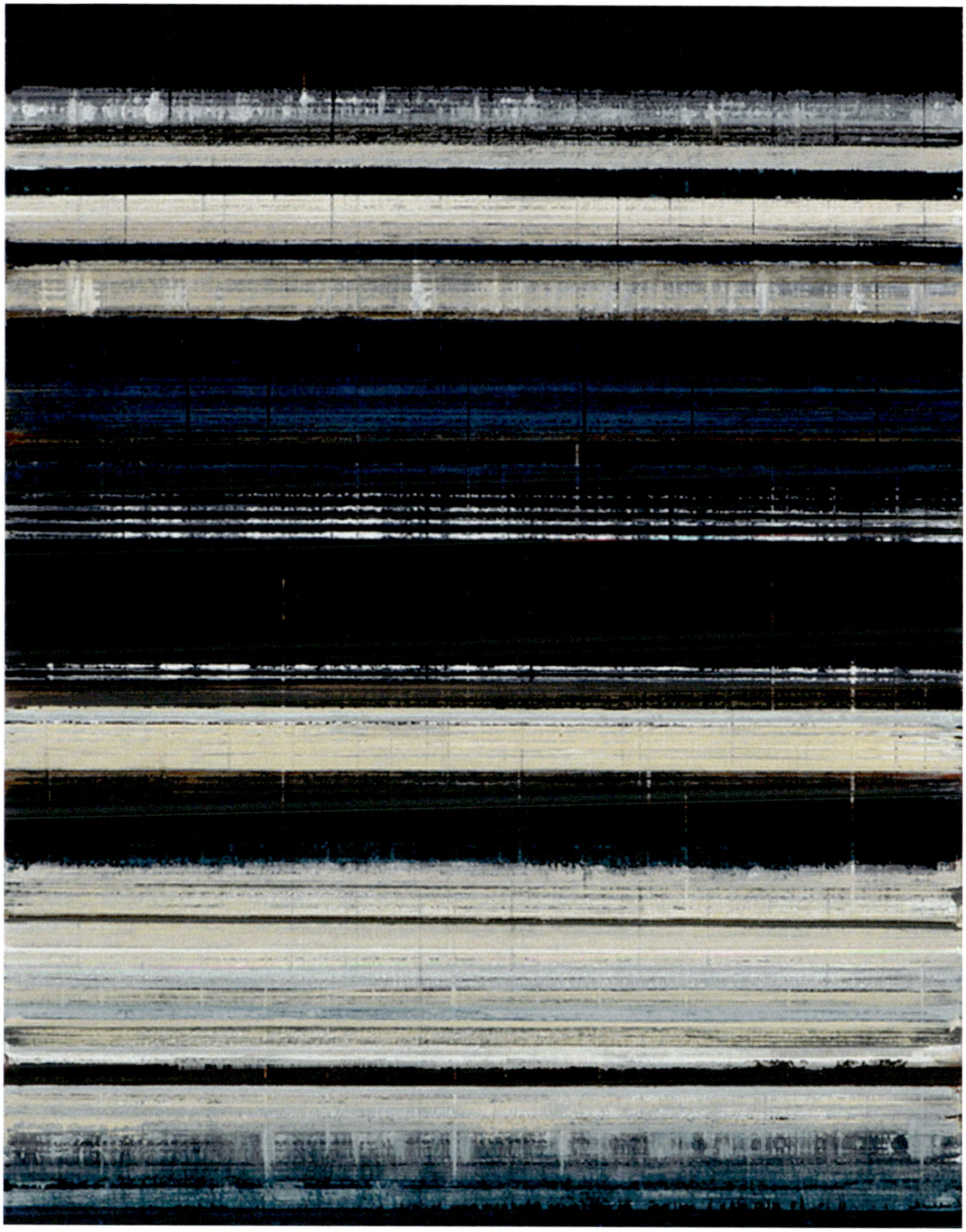

Leah Oates

T*ransitory Space,*
Prospect Park, Brooklyn
Winter 2014
Color Photograph

11 in x 14 in

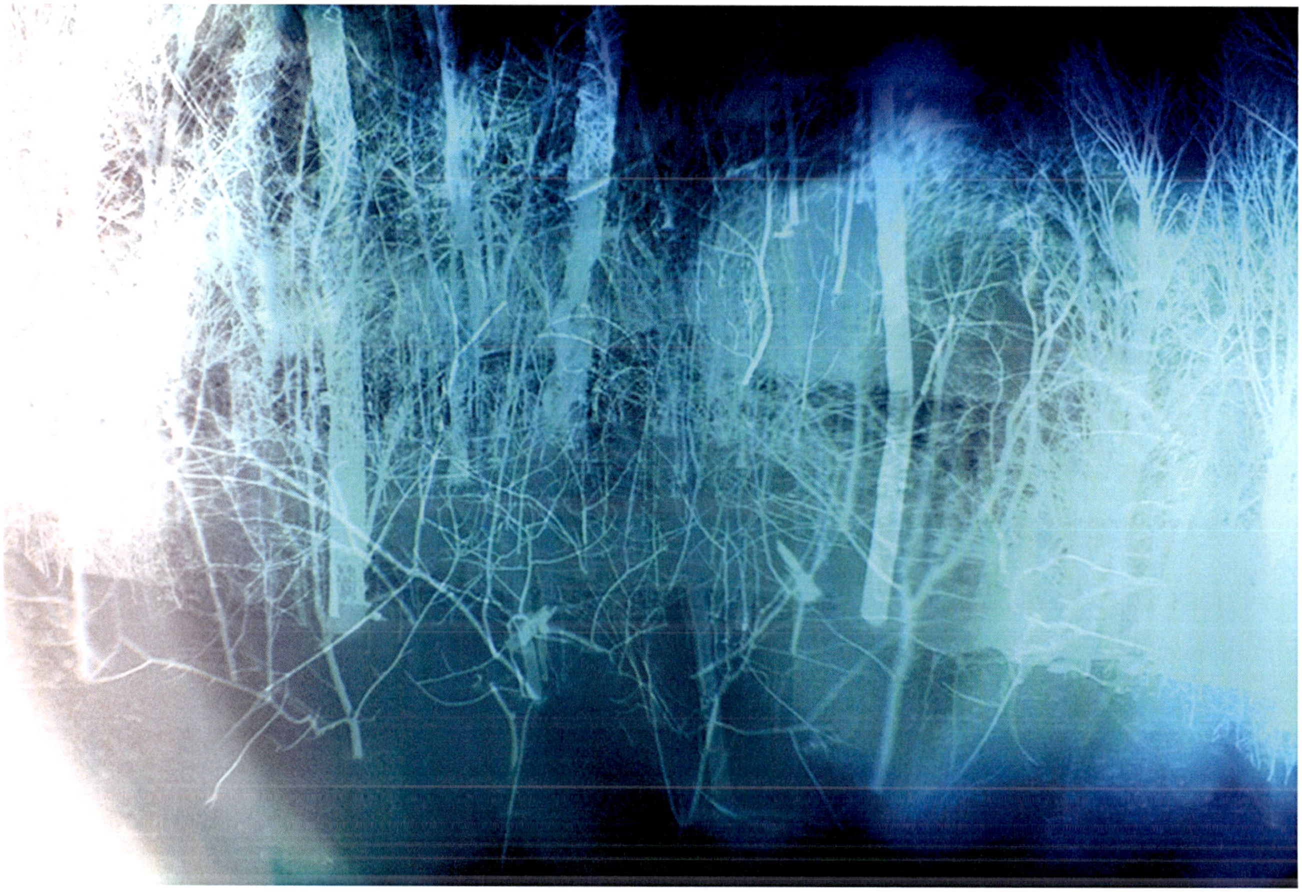

Leah Oates

T*ransitory Space,*
Prospect Park, Brooklyn
Winter 2014
Color Photograph

11 in x 14 in

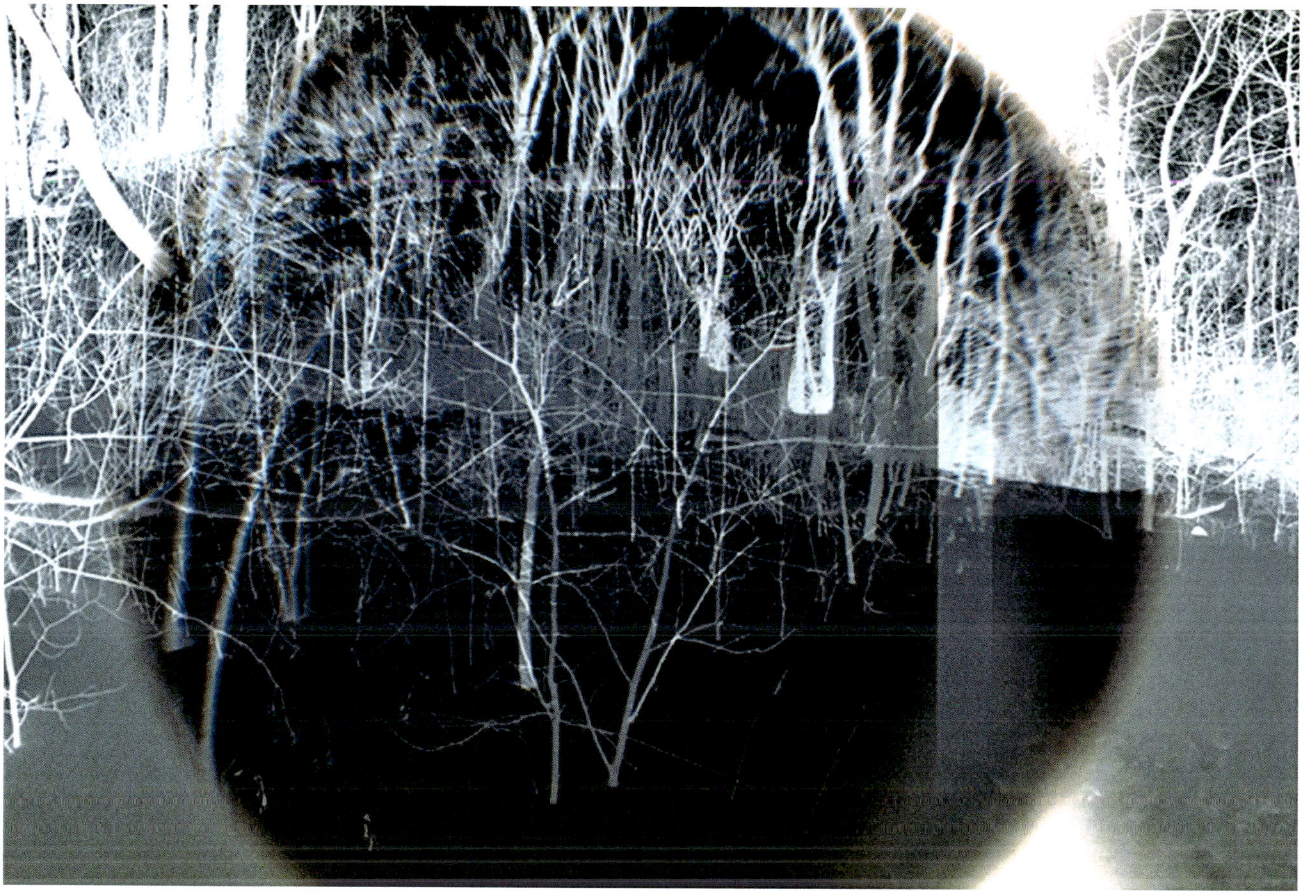

Ann-Marie Cunningham

Hoarfrost

Digital Photograph

8.5 in x 11 in

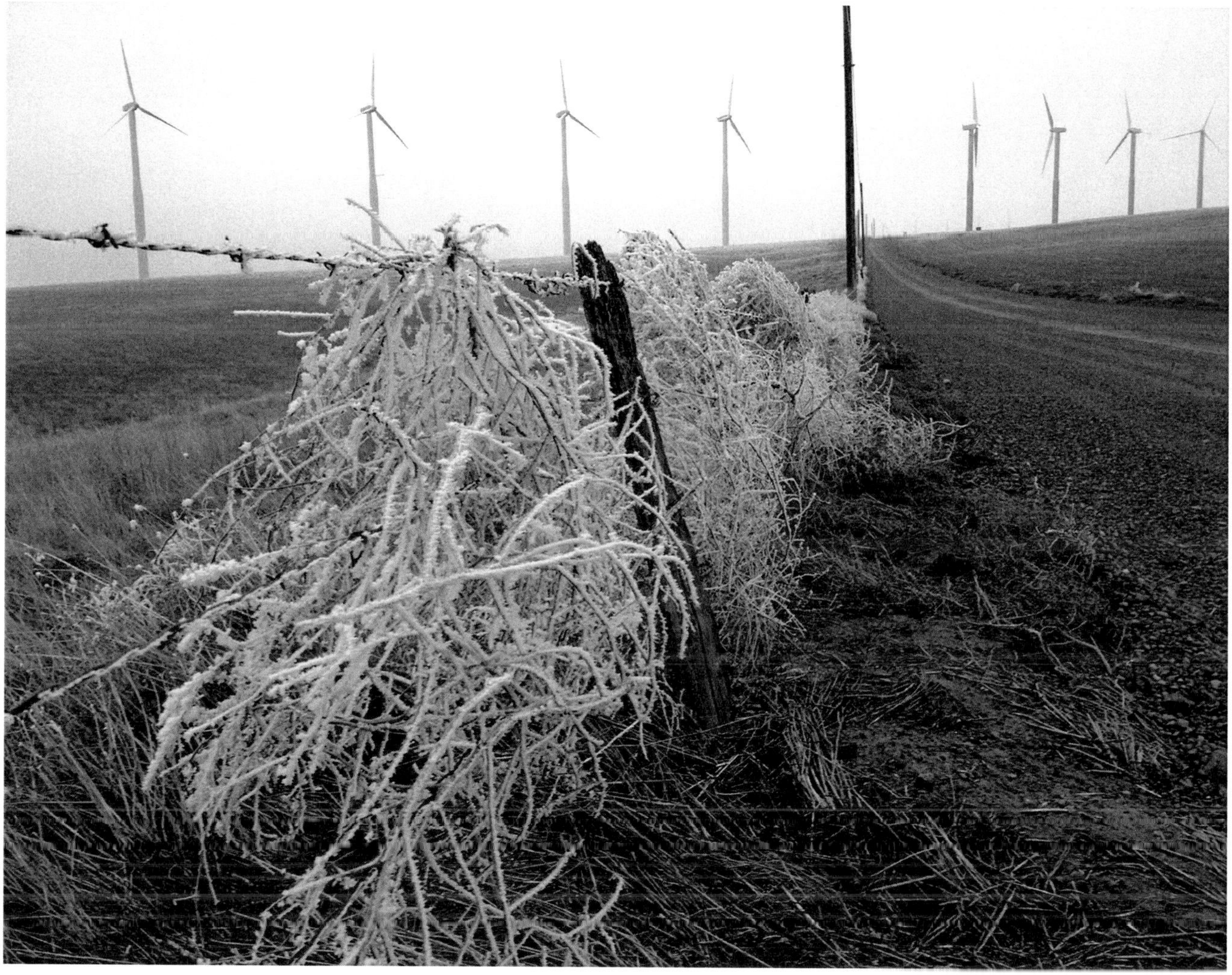

Hoarfrost
By Ann-Marie Cunningham

air and ground transpire
frigid phenomena bares
white crystalline barbs

Danielle Austen

Barrier 2

Archival Pigment Print

24 in x 16 in

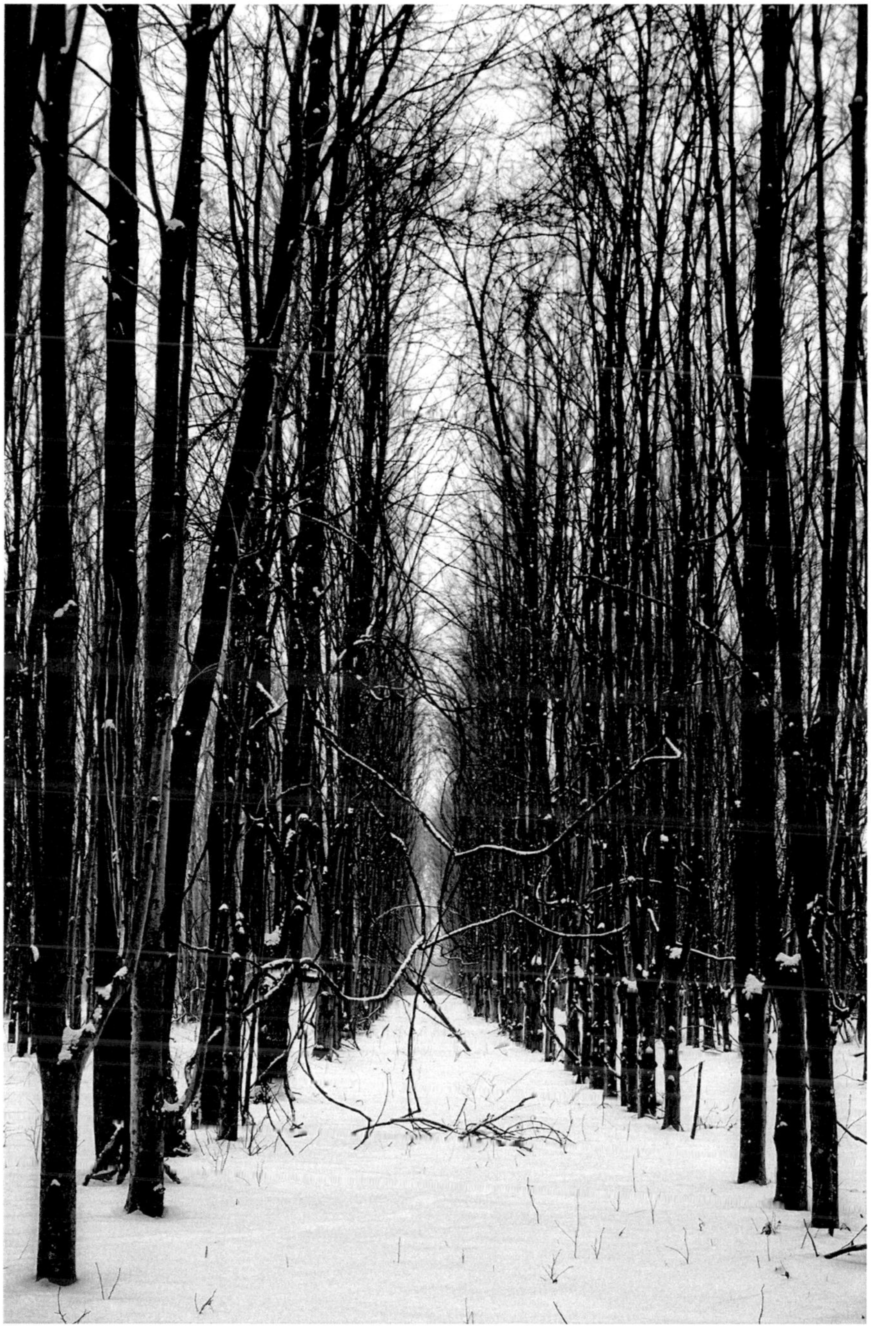

Danielle Austen

Ice Flame

Archival Pigment Print

15 in x 20 in

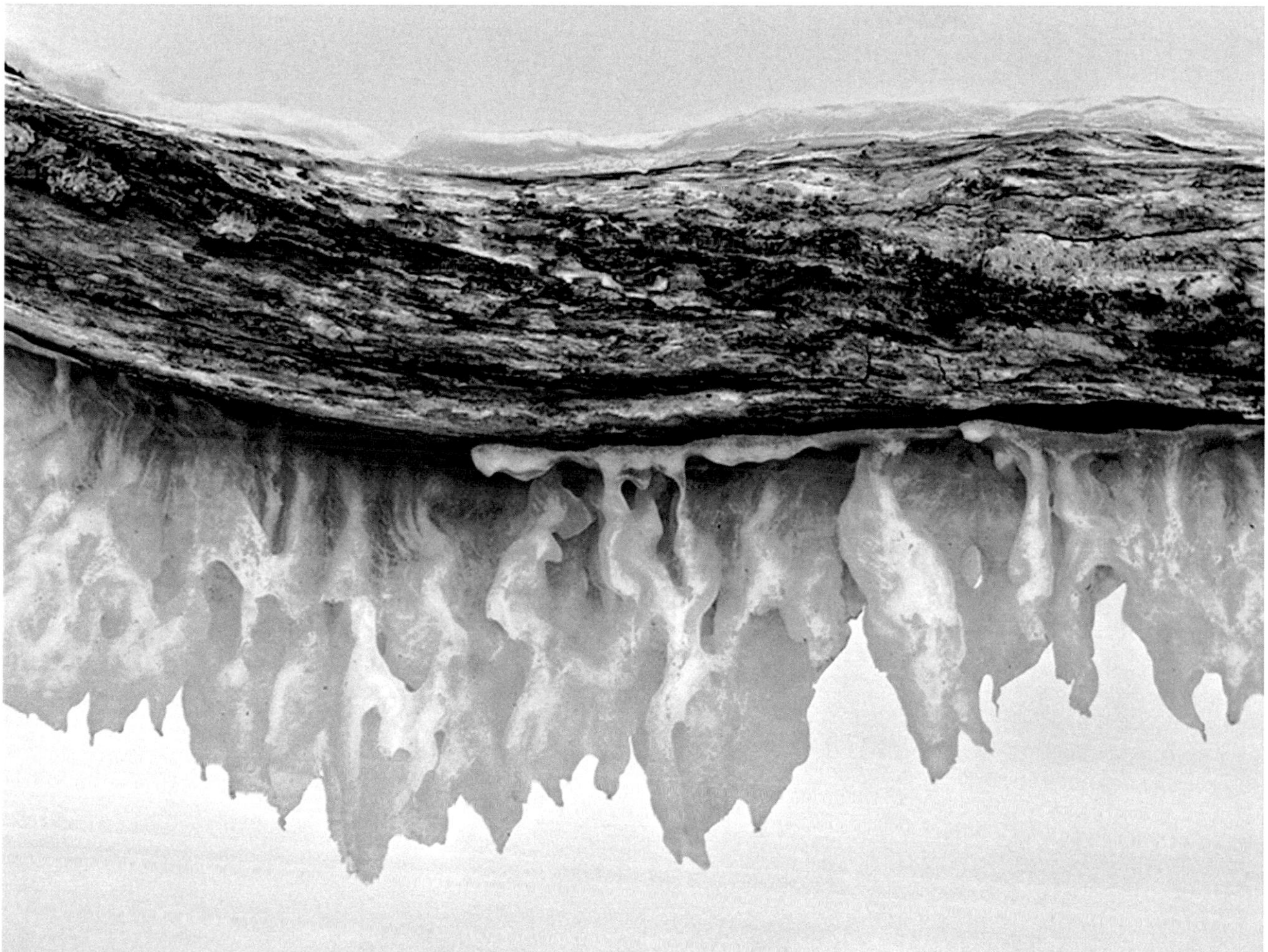

Danielle Austen

Frozen Tide

Archival Pigment Print

14 in x 27 in

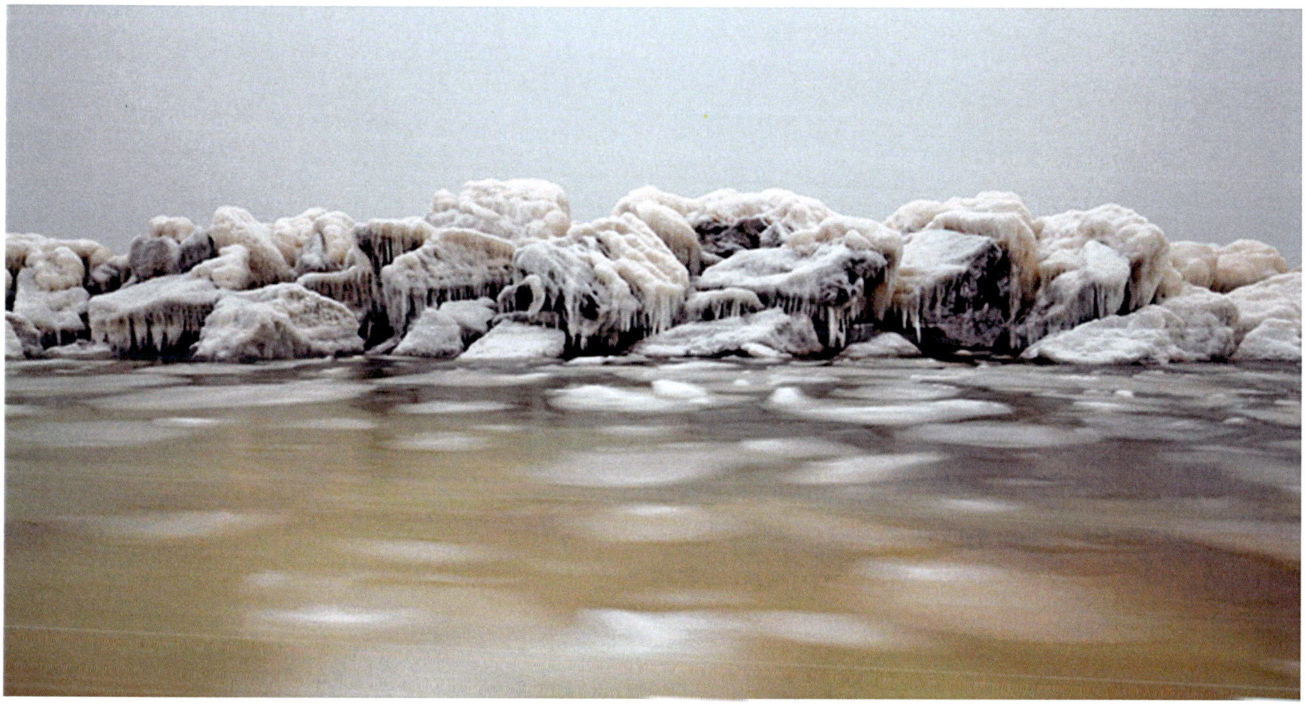

Aspetto Esterno
By Ashley Busby

Somewhere,
in each second,
is a dark line,
an open syllable that lies awake.
Dust-green dusk,
the quiet breath of the world,
it used to haunt me,
and some days, it still does.
Absence of earth,
the weeds of myth,
finding a half-truth
clipped back
cupped within my hands.

Waiting,
for that infinite sound,
Who is it
that fills us with silence?
Pressed into the light,
the common ancestor
Obsidian
with small eyes,
cuffing his sleeves
Nothing is nothing is nothing,
the structure is shifting,
wanting to know.

Ashley Busby

Residual

Oil and Gesso on Masonite

24 in x 48 in

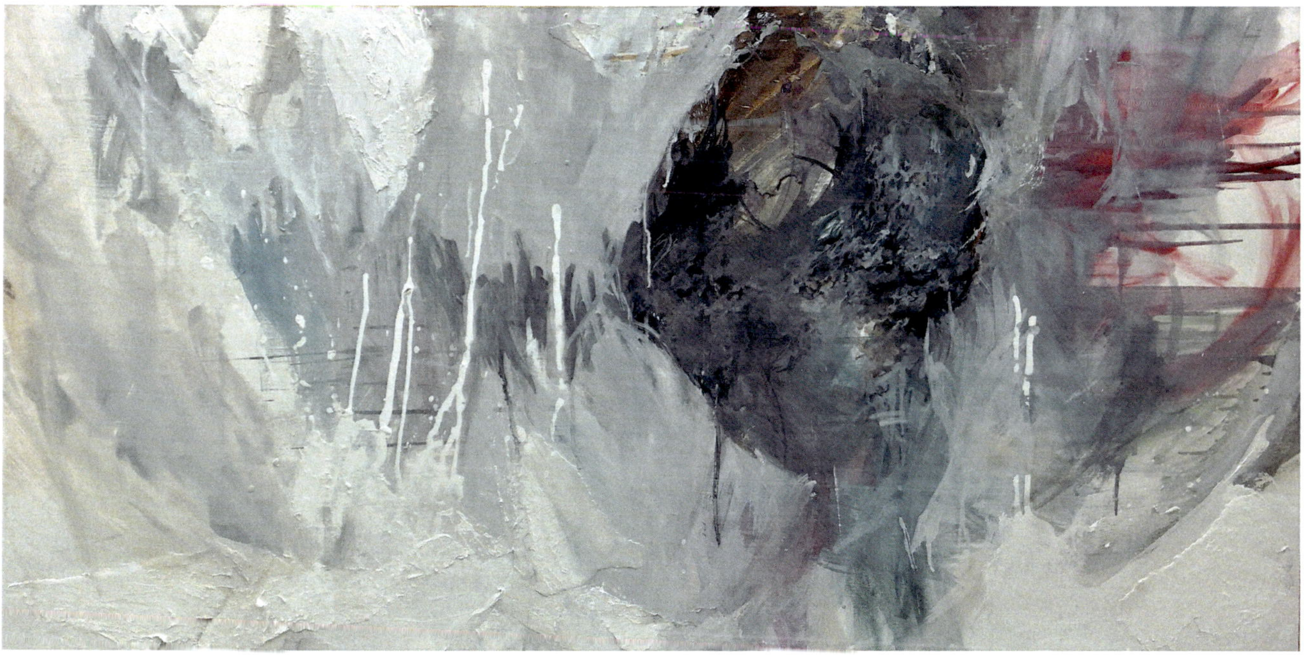

Dahlia

By Ashley Busby

Twelve days
Her palm like an open star,
and we step into place.
Looking and looking away
from that small dark world
with no frame.
Tonight we forget
and become strangers.
Be still, he says,
There is something more brilliant out there

Underneath the fire,
the mystic breathes
her blue smoke dream.
Cursive and cursed,
a memory of a memory.
The end of surrender,
your hand against mine,
brushing away sighs
and shadows from the sun,
into another dream.

James Boychuk-Hunter

Stacked Hay

Photo Etching

49 in x 36 in

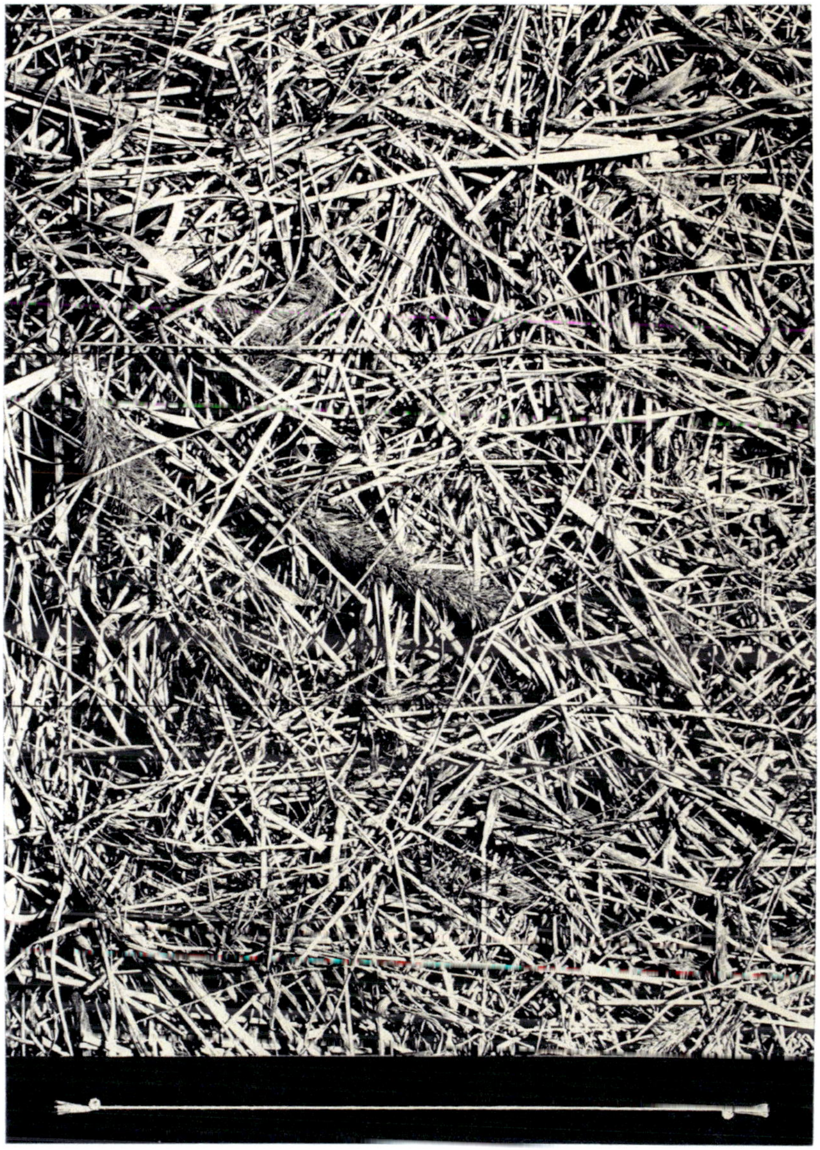

James Boychuk-Hunter

Stacked Ginkgo

Photo Etching

52 in x 35 in

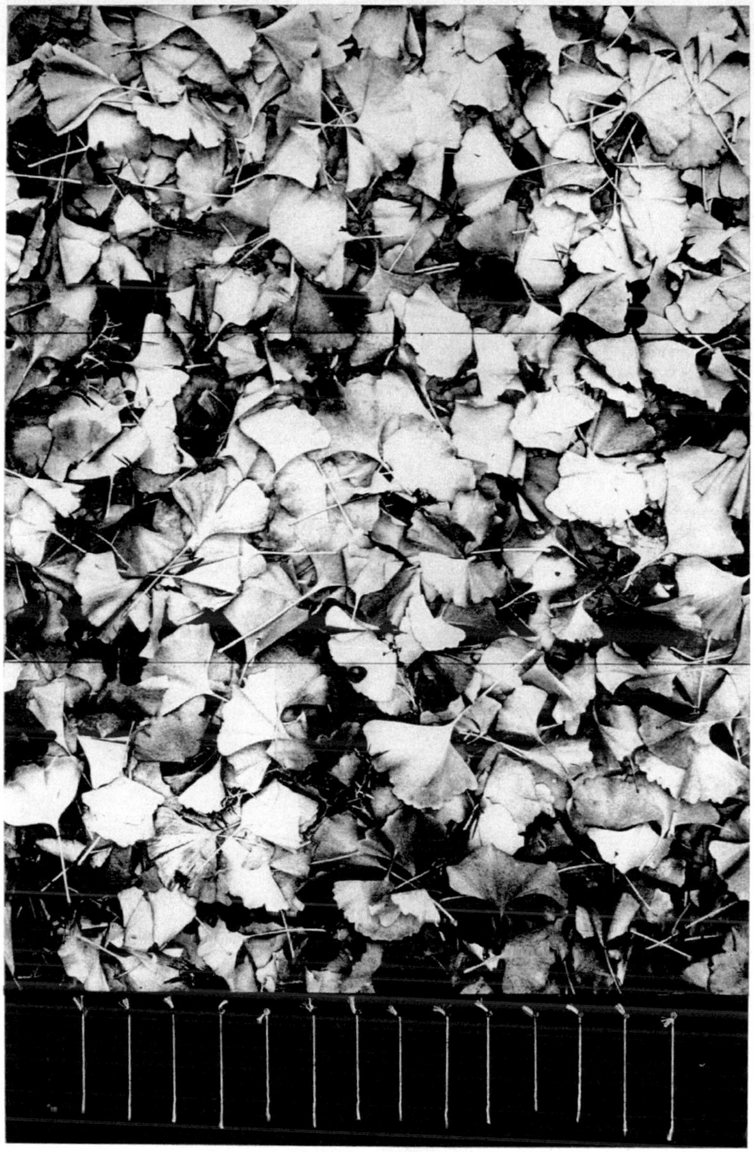

Carla Shapiro

Nothing But Remarkable

Platinum/palladium print

8 in x 8 in

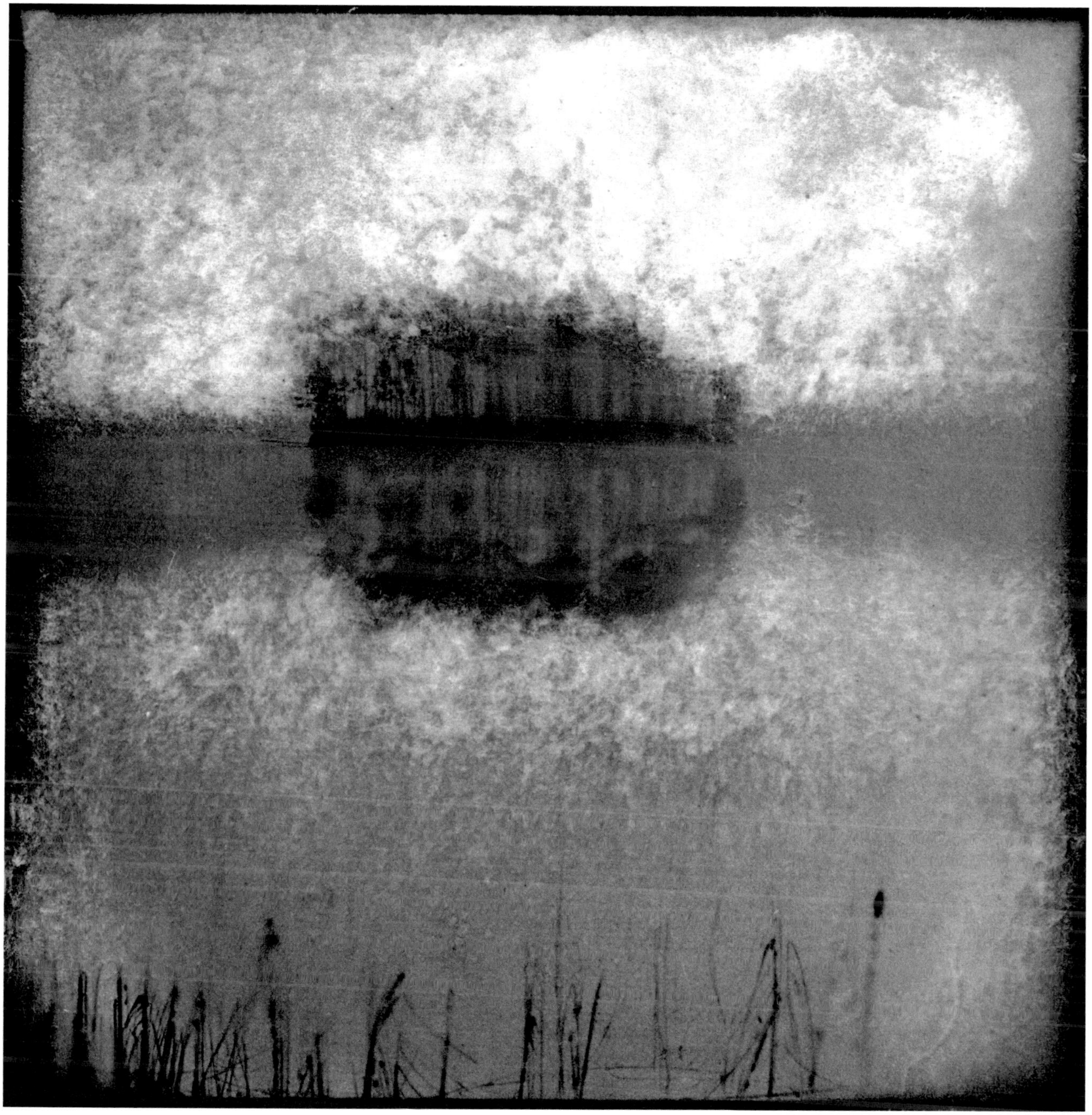

Carla Shapiro

Moments Later

Platinum/palladium print

8 in x 8 in

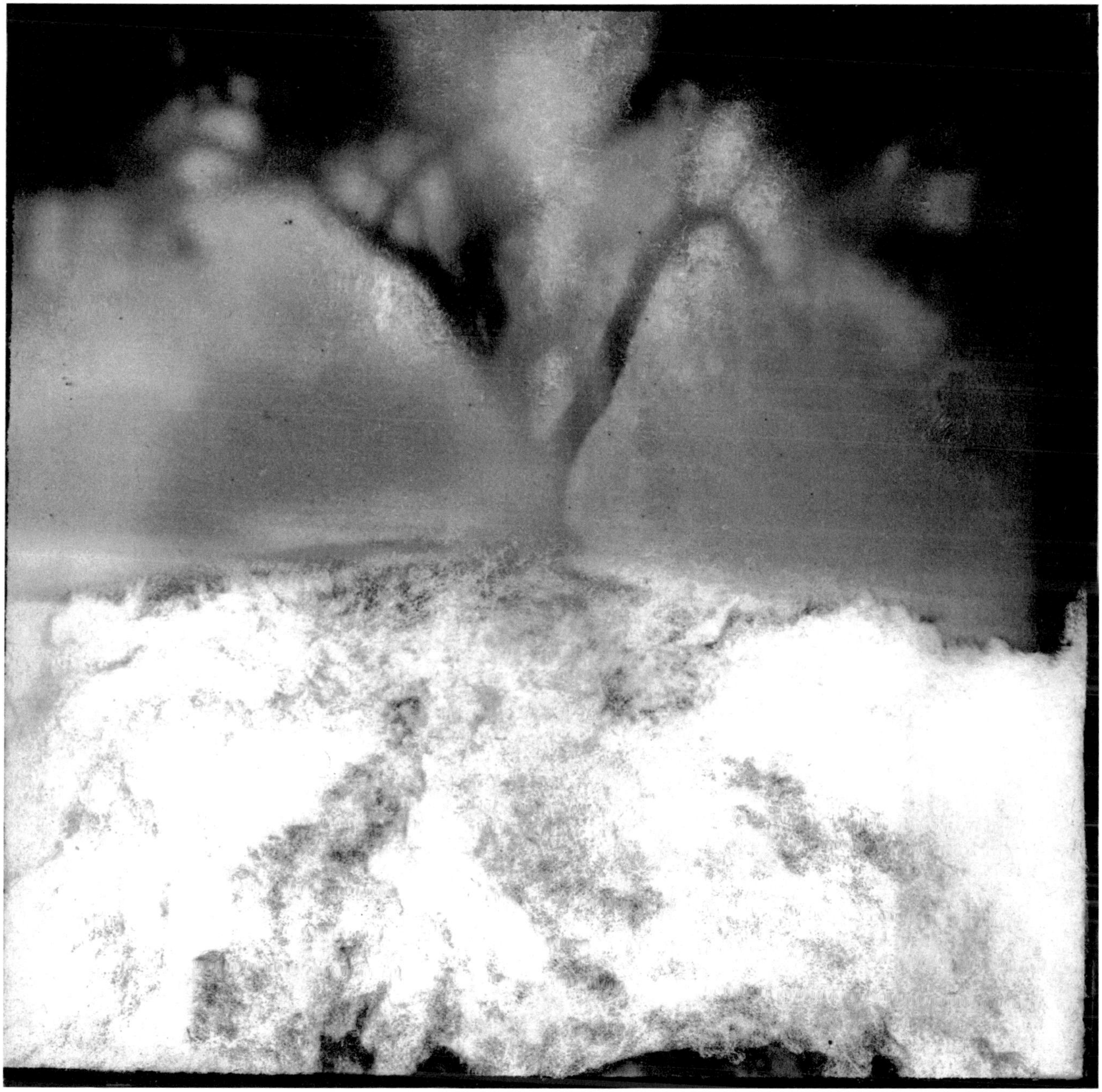

Carla Shapiro

Wait

Platinum/palladium print

8 in x 8 in

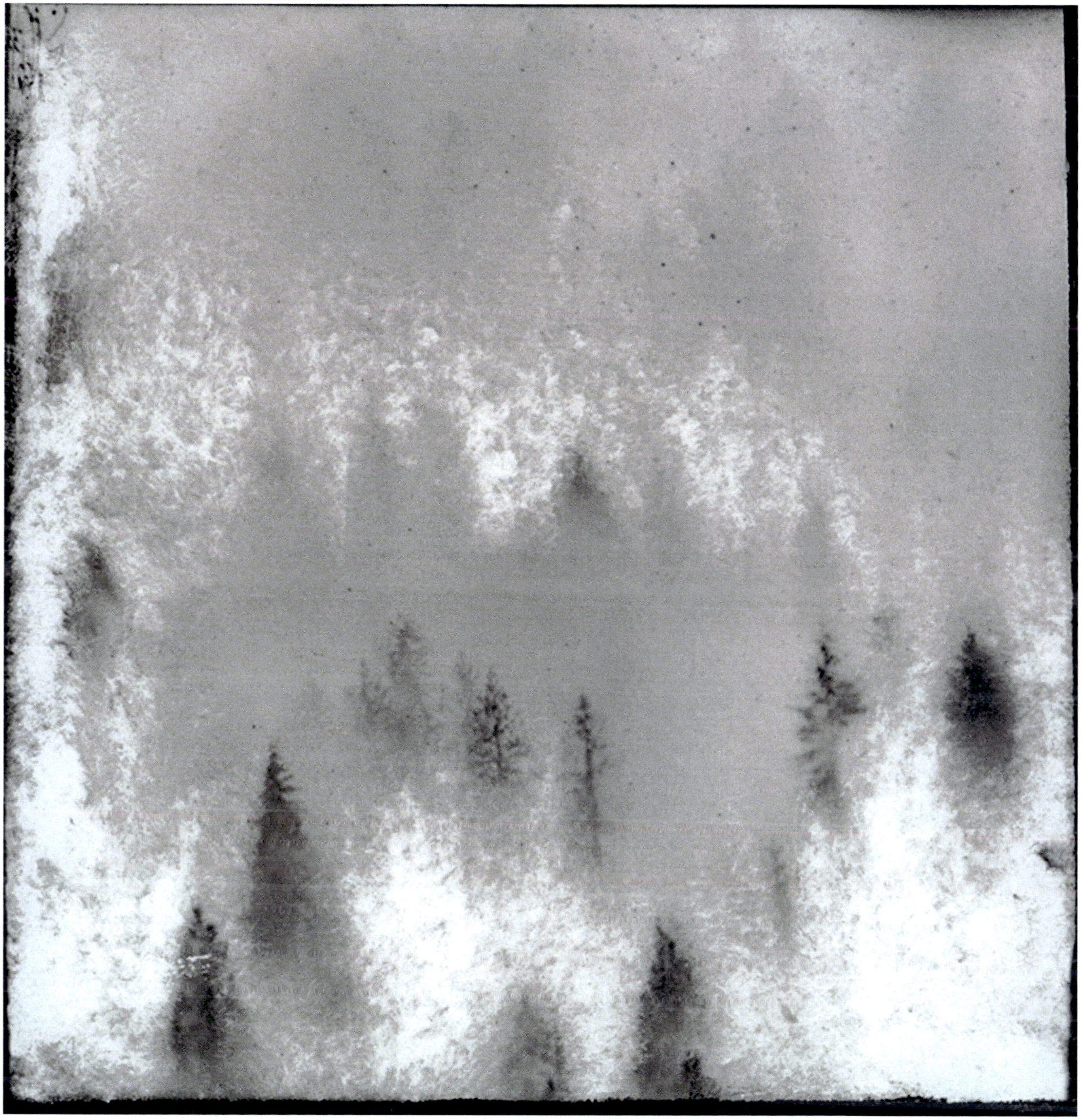

Carla Shapiro

That is Not True

Platinum/palladium print

8.5 in x 8 in

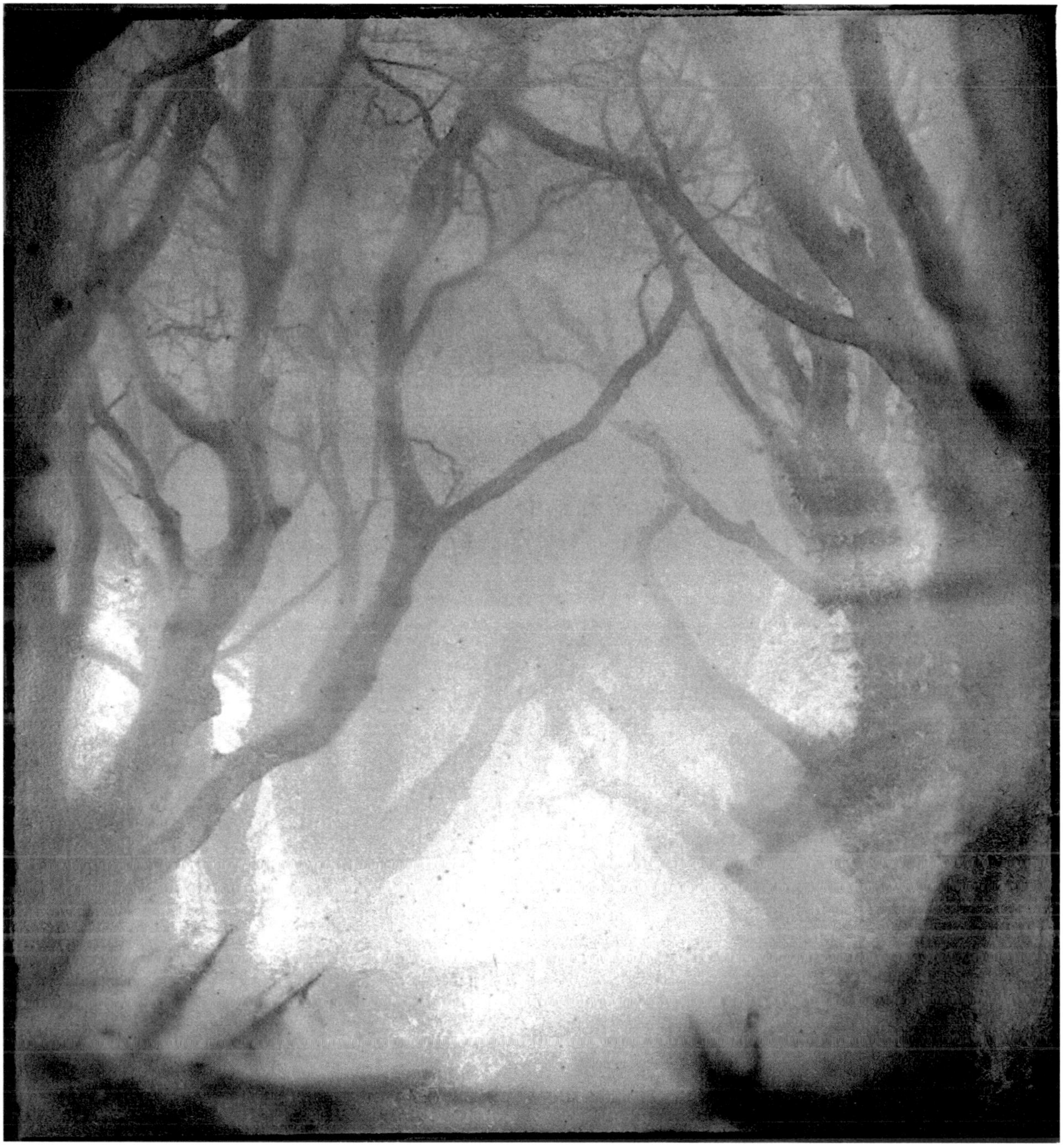

Ira Upin

Lonely Road

Oil, Acrylic, Spray Enamel,
Maps on Panel

43 in x 41 in

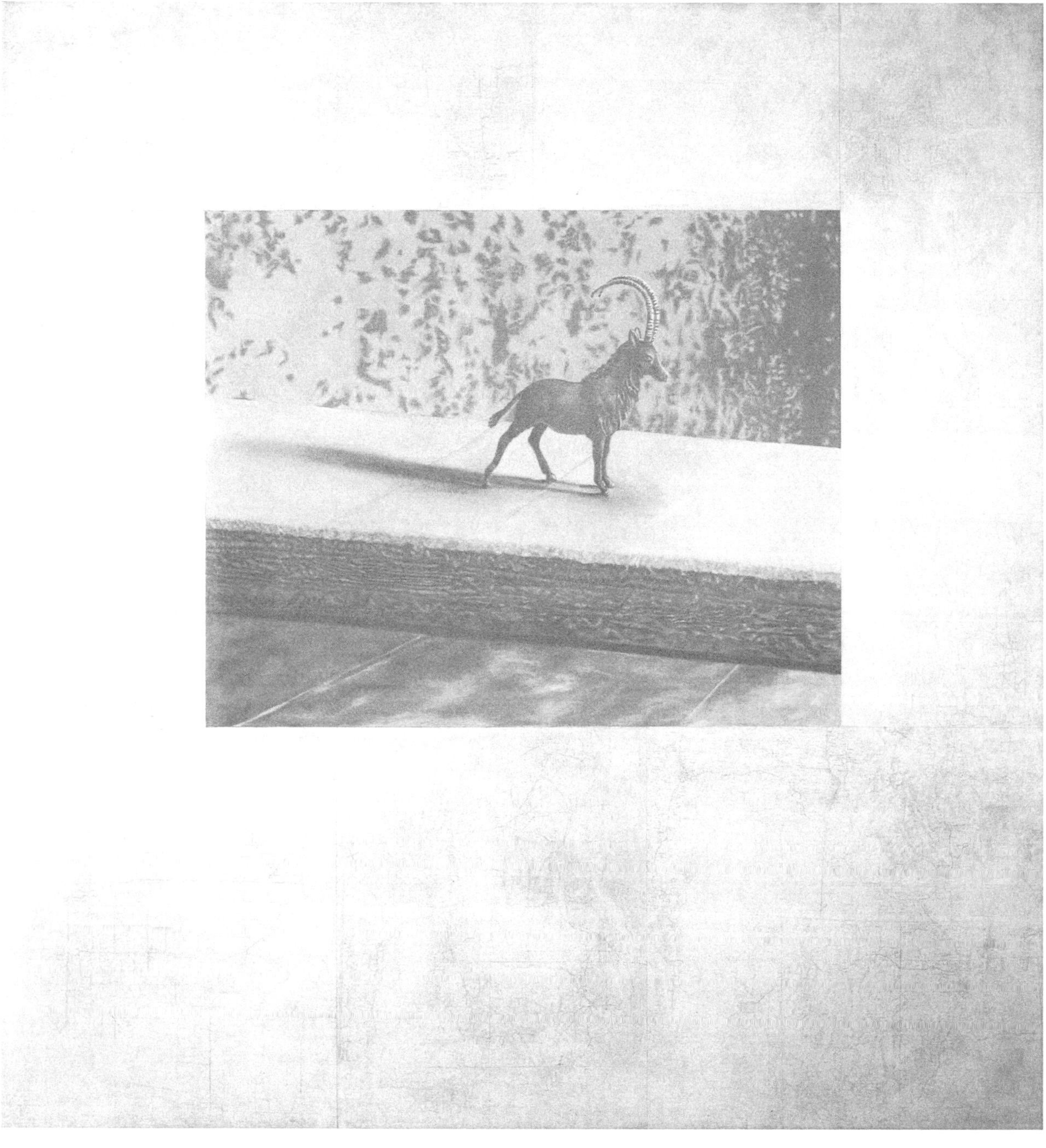

Ryn Clarke

Three Sentinels

Digital Ink Photograph

20 in x 30 in

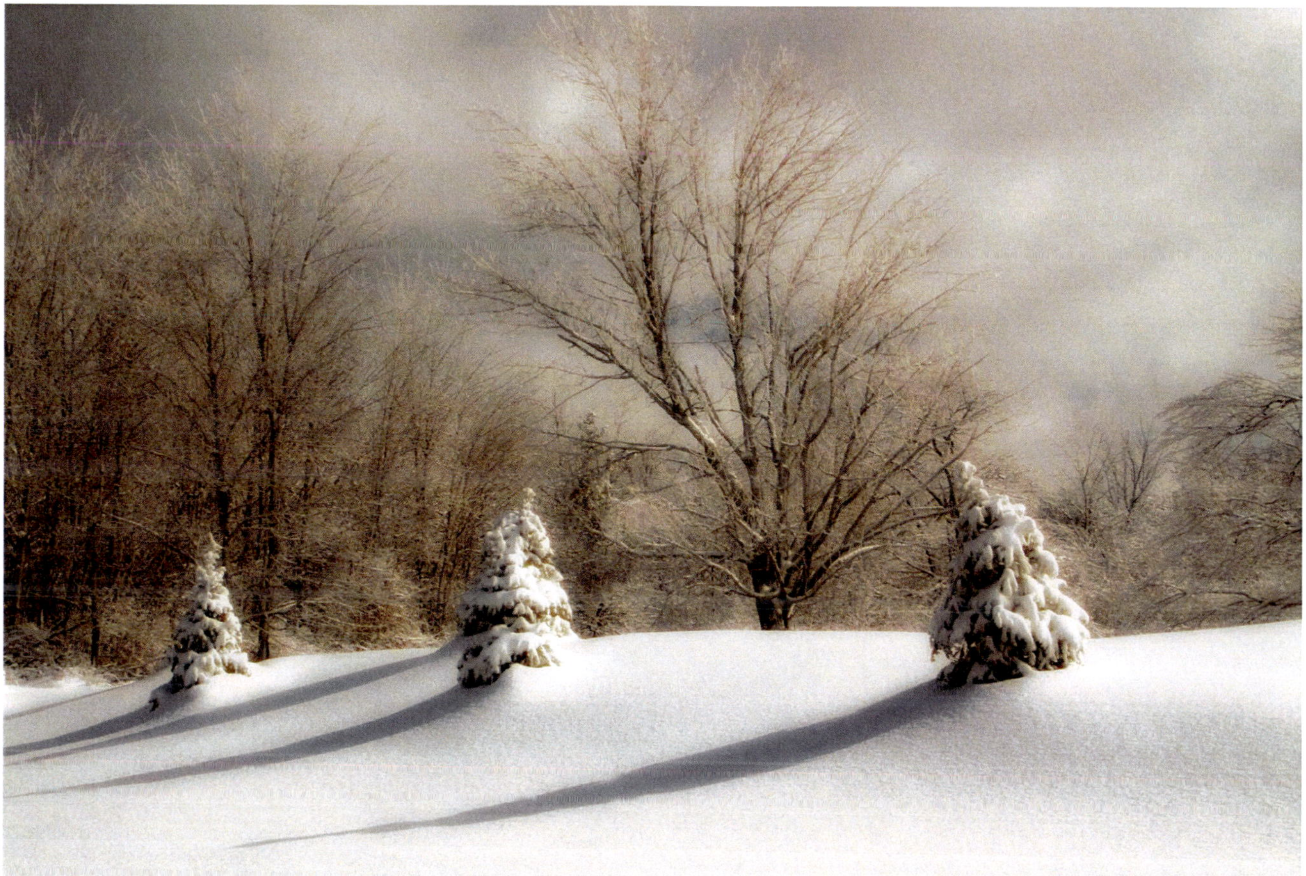

Ryn Clarke

Chinese Maple

Digital Ink Photograph

12.5 in x 9.5 in

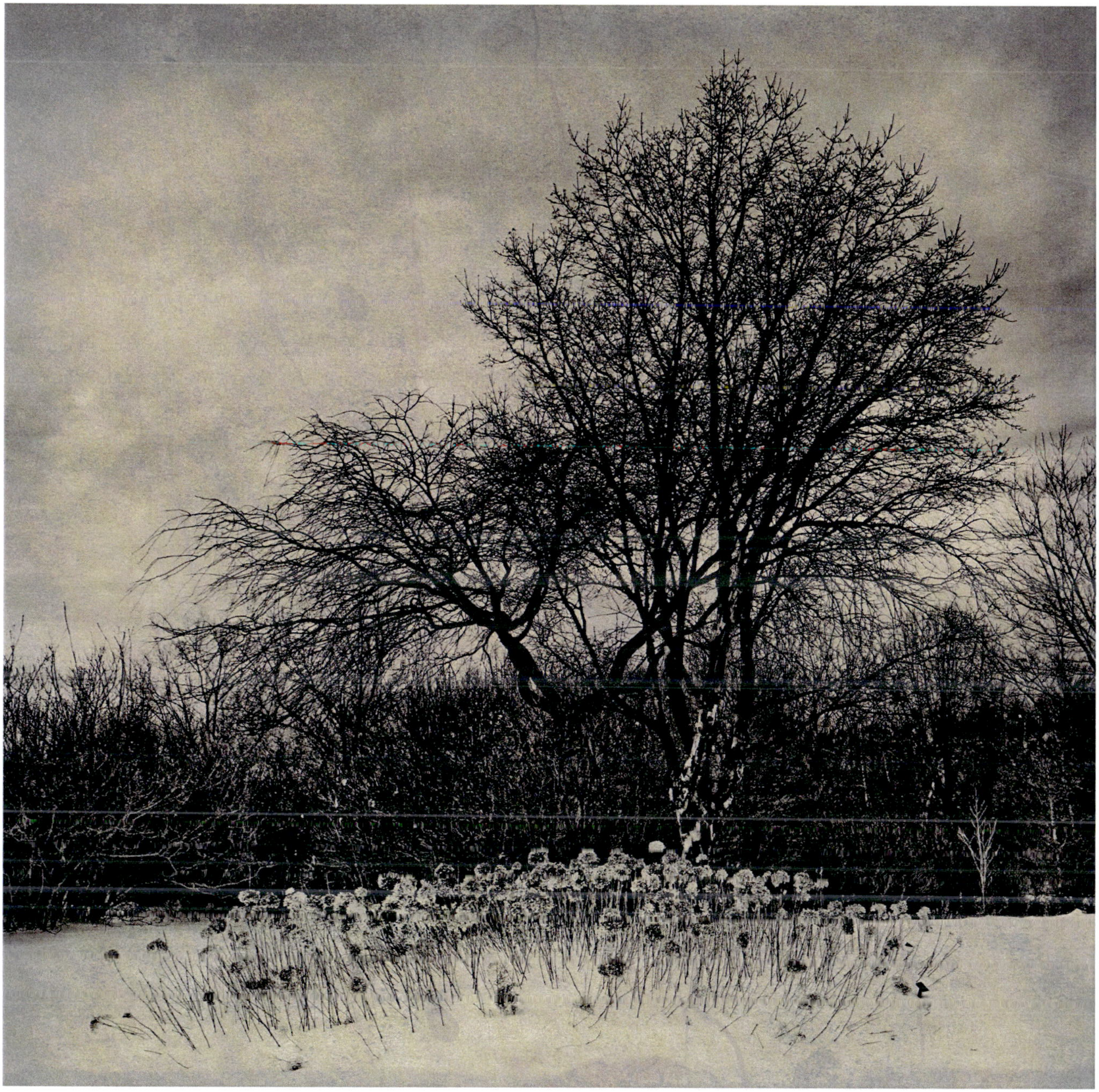

Ryn Clarke

Cattails in Snow

Digital Ink Photograph

12.5 in x 9.5 in

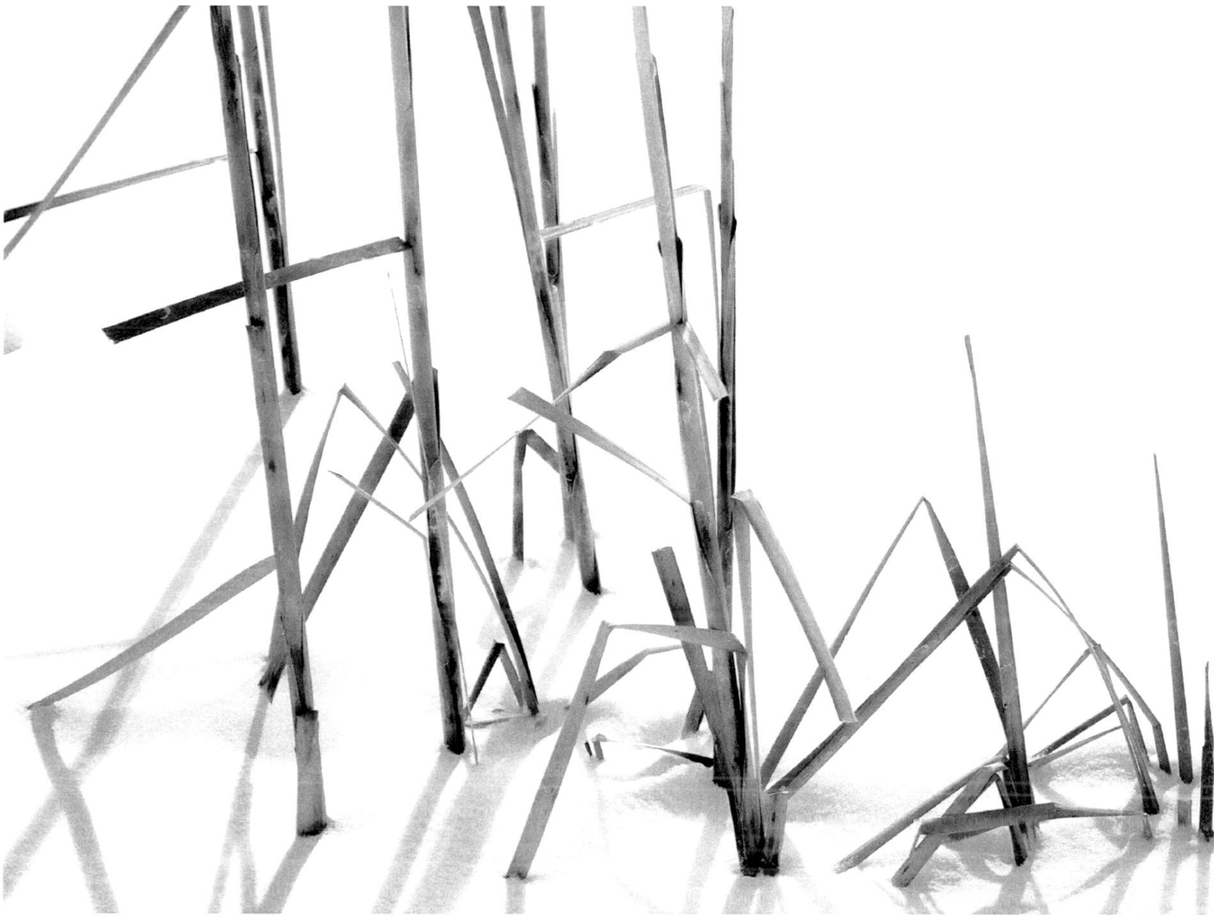

Ryn Clarke

Two Pink Ribbons

Digital Ink Photograph

30 in x 20 in

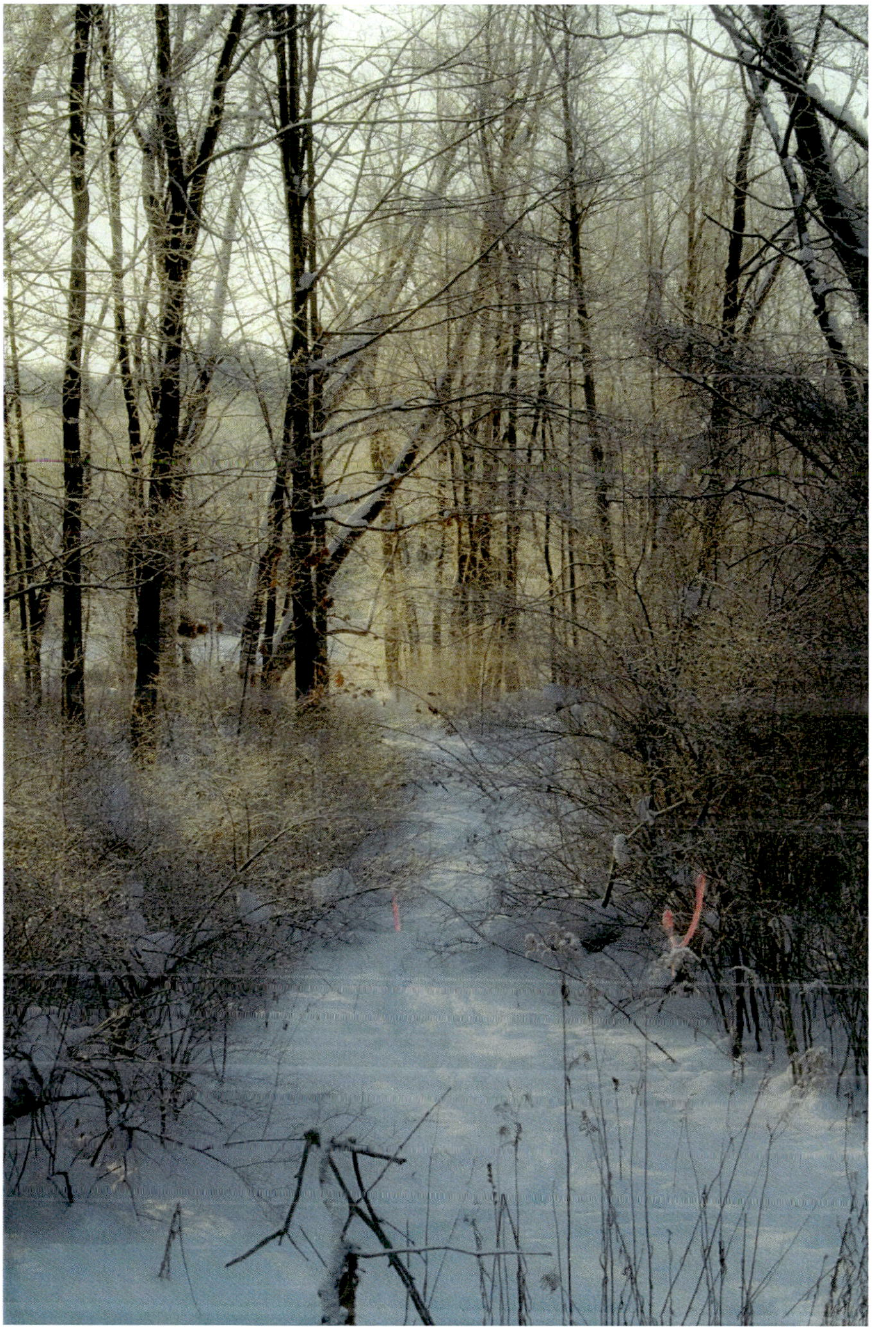

By Mark Needham

Snow is no burden
to the horse wearing cold; it's
lighter than a fly.

Mark Needham

Fortuna in Snow

Photograph

10.5 in x 5.25 in

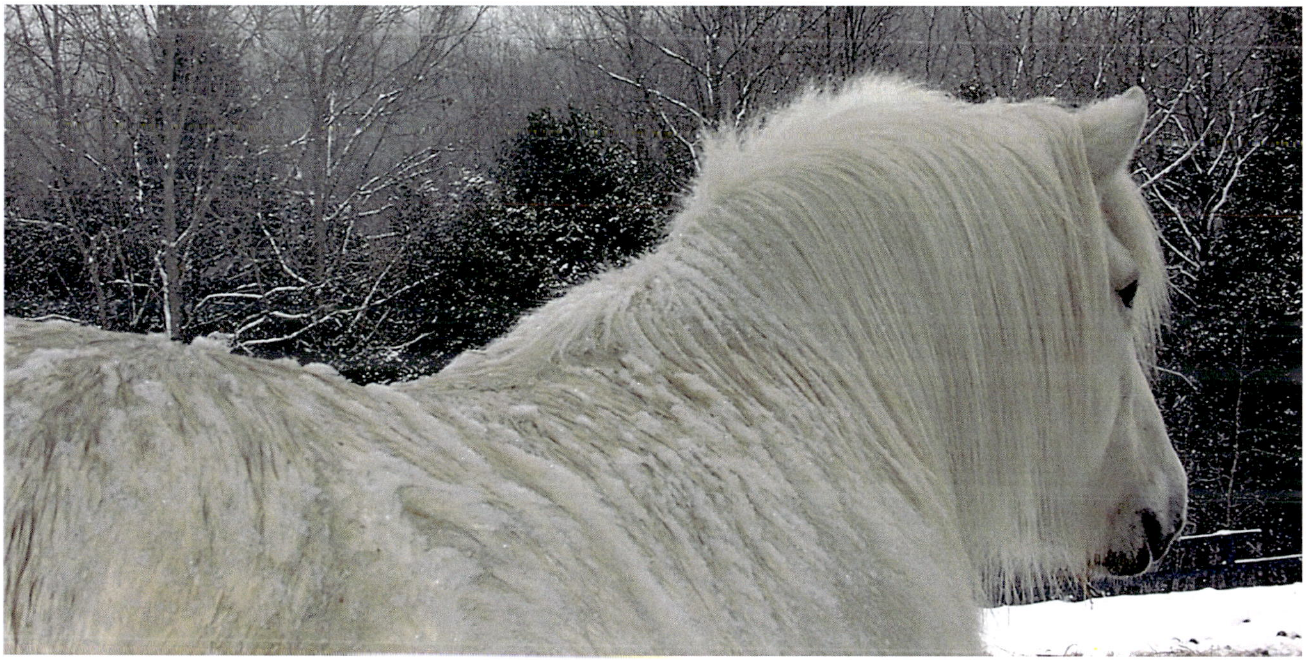

By Mark Needham

There is art in ice…
air frozen in poetry,
explosions at rest.

Mark Needham

Icy Twig

Photograph

10 in x 6.3 in

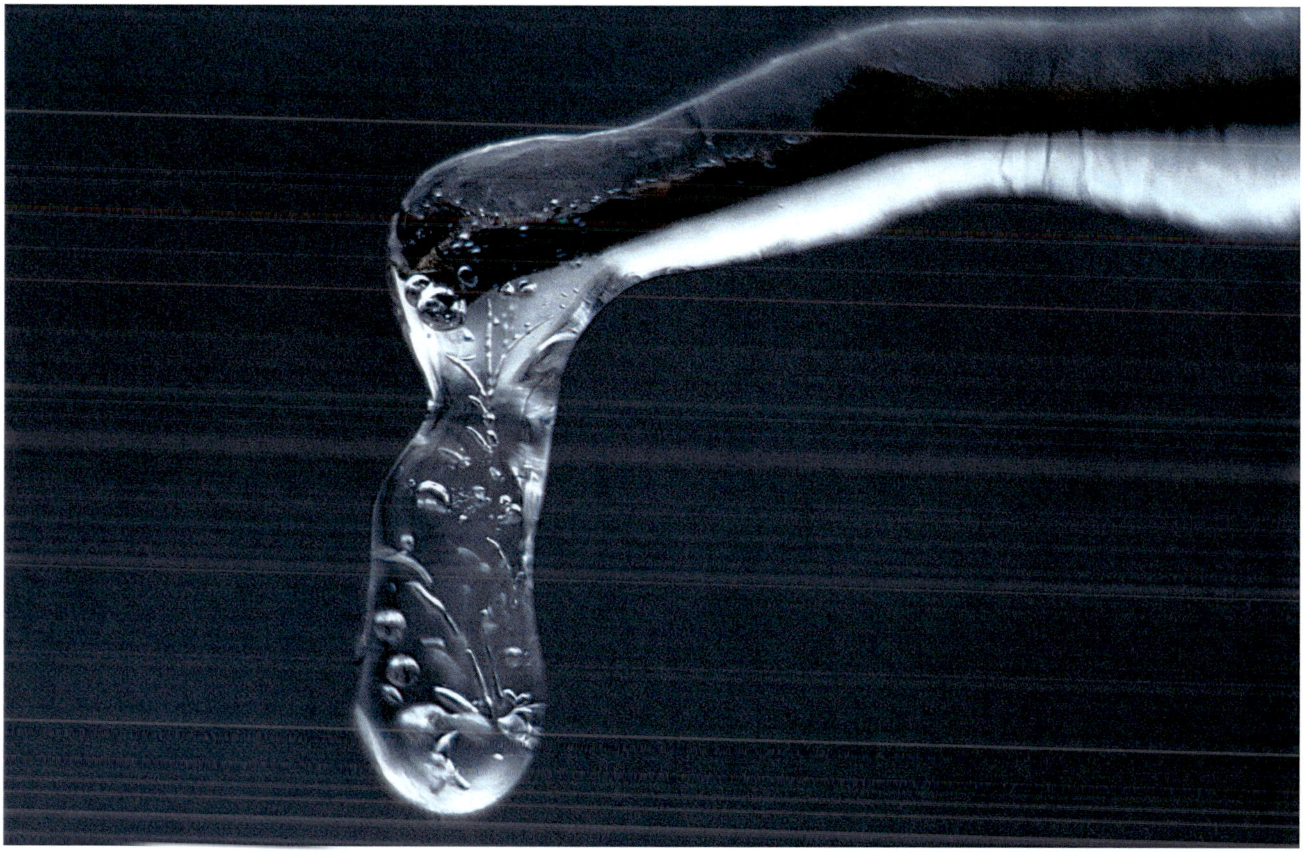

Pamela Rogers

Protected from Sleet

Graphite, carbon, ink, plant pigments

30 in x 22 in

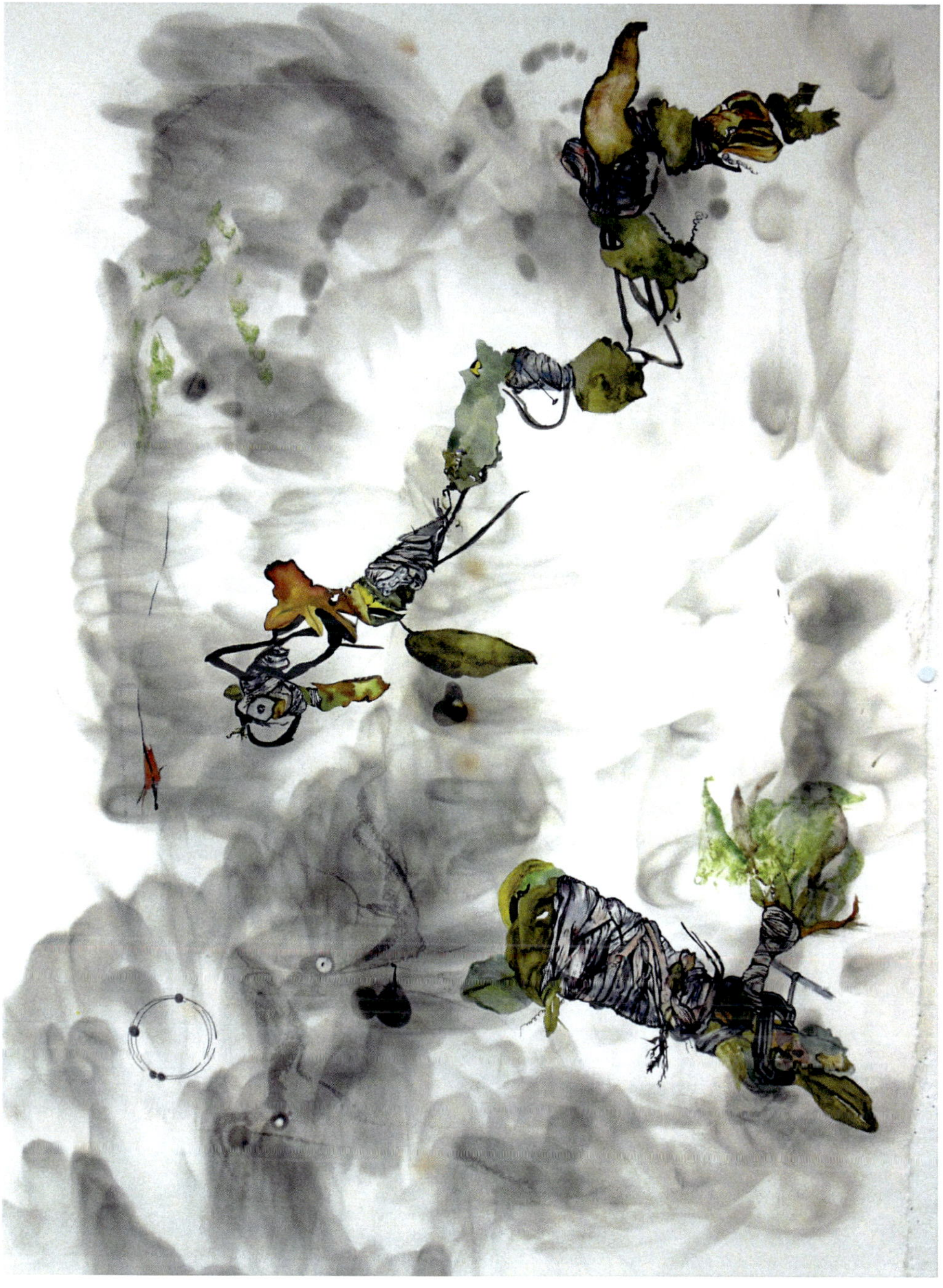

Pamela Rogers

Meadow Muse #2

Graphite, minerals pigment
on artist made paper

16in x 11 in

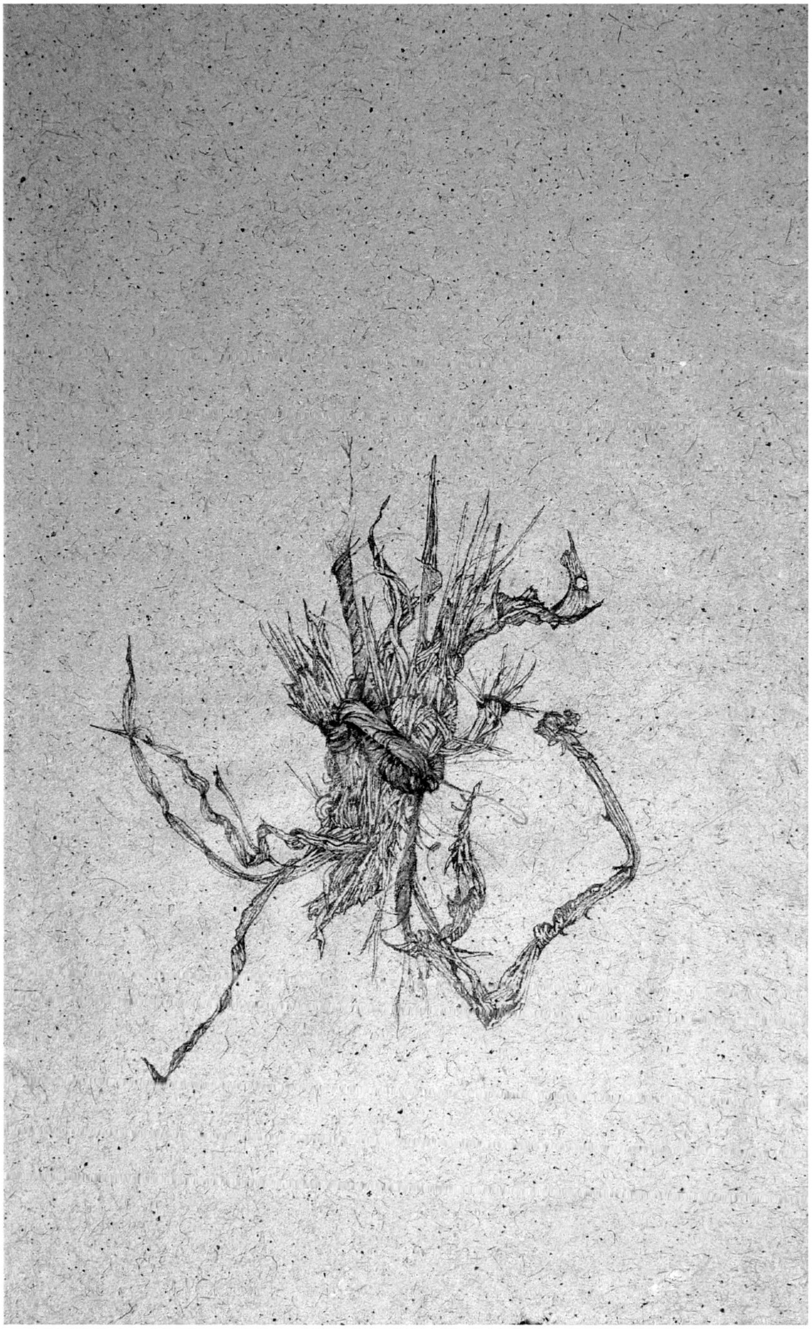

Pamela Rogers

Snow Day

soil and mineral pigments,
graphite and in

30 in x 22 in

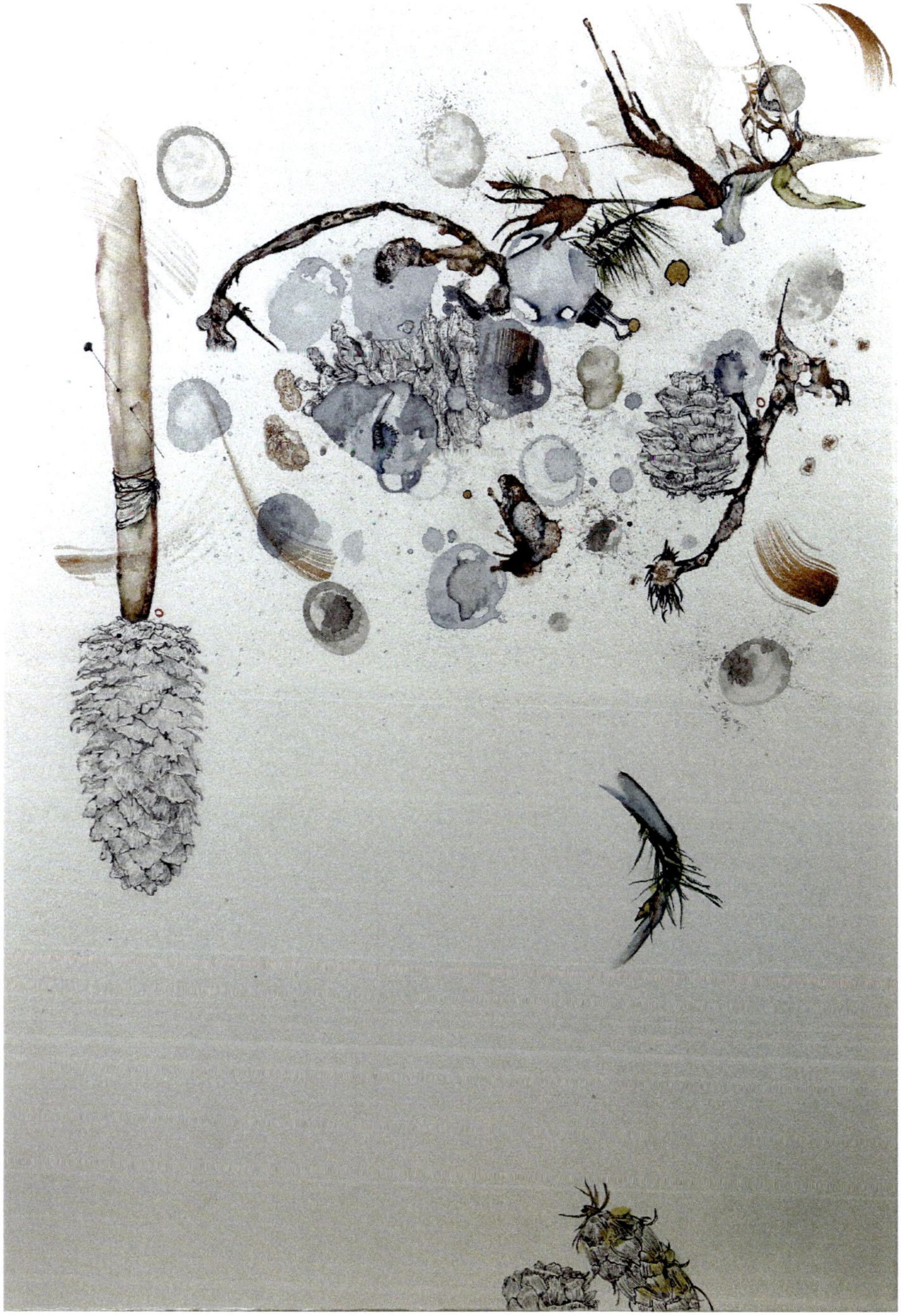

Of Winter

By Jillian Breitfeller

When I say you are
of winter I say it with
fire in my soul-
the words are warm
on my breath and
the surrounding air
melts into gentle
spinning song.
You, the crystallized quiet
of blanketed snow;
of inspiration that
comes only
in purity in gifts
from the sky.

The shedding
so I grow-
the withering that is
not sorrow so as to
be reborn;
at once the cloak
around my delicacy,
and the taste of
clean cold on
thirsty tongue.
With glistening eyes
you plant seeds
in the soon ready earth,
feeding them with your
light, sowing their
trust in temporary darkness.
You, my Divine.
Of winter, we won't need-
for we are the sun.

Carole Boyd

Winter Walk

Digital Painting

16 in x 16 in

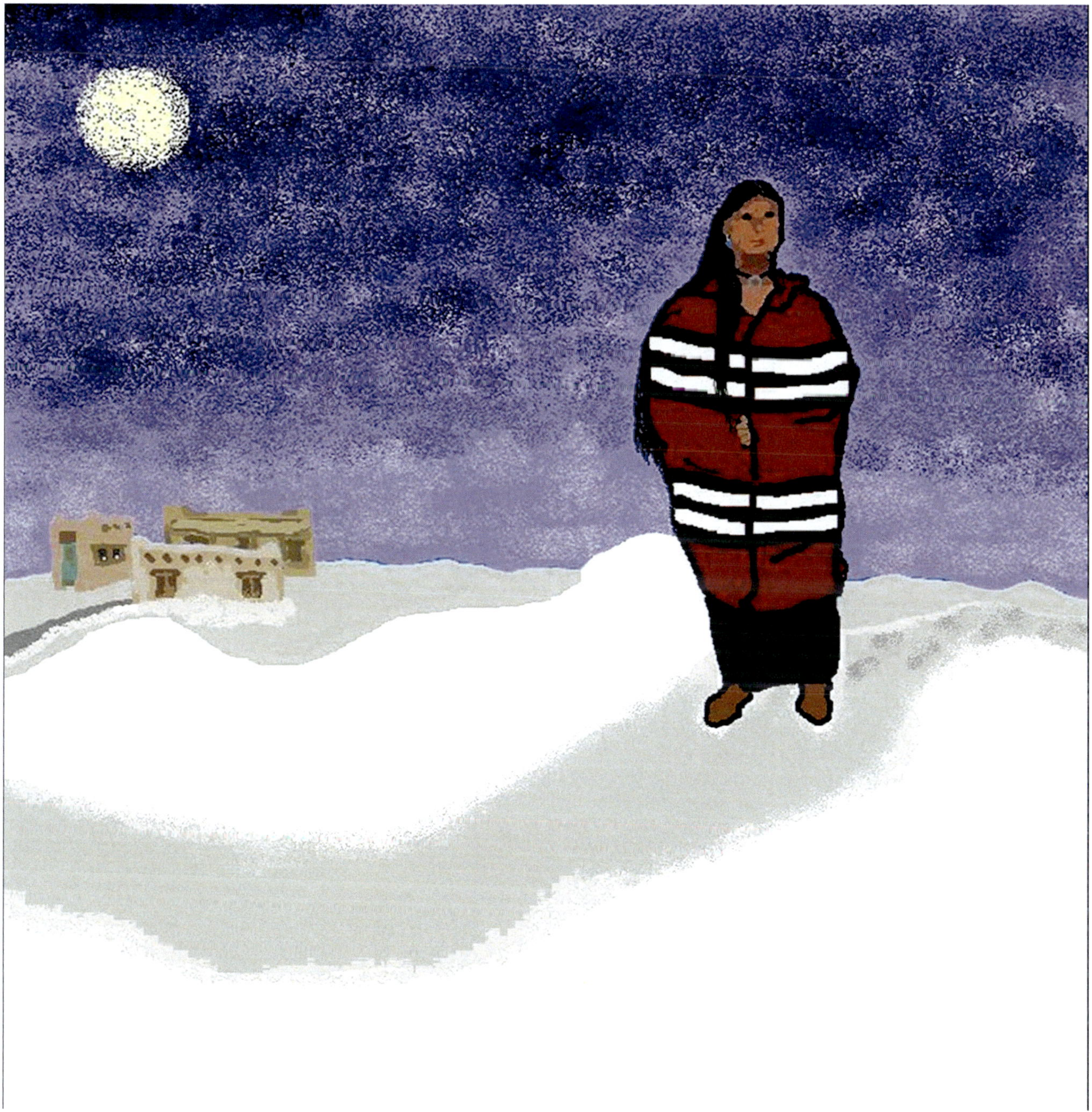

Carole Boyd

Deer in Snow

Digital Painting

10 in x 14 in

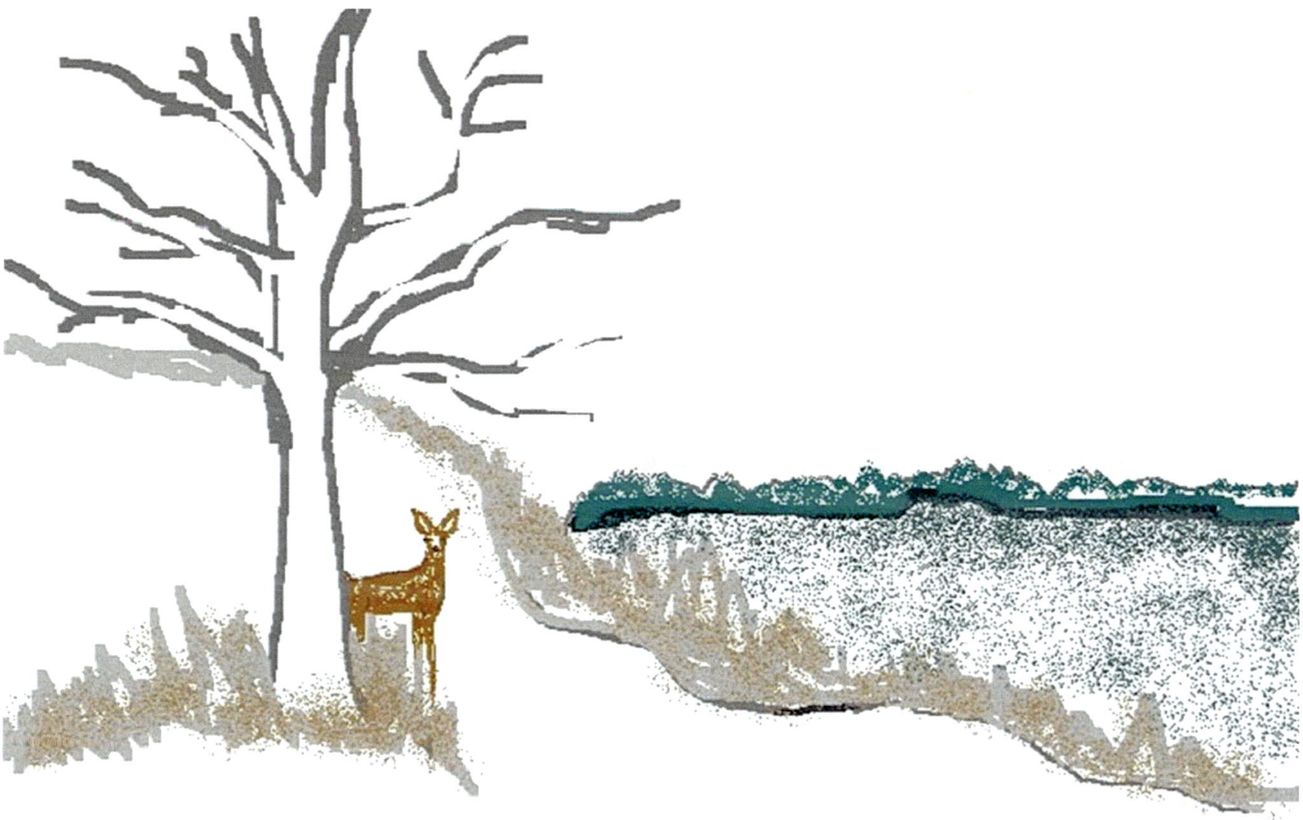

The Land

By Pamela Herron

the land
a living, breathing place

mirrors the cycles of woman

birth and blossom
rites of fertility
fulfillment of harvest

respite still
quietness of a long winter
a little death

rest and rejuvenation
a spring of rebirth
holding the seeds of life

on our farm
I walked every fence-line
hauled firewood, planted, harvested

year in
and year out
planting by the moon

farms lay over the hills
a rumpled patchwork
of our labors

brooding trees watch
stewards of our house
to the next county

when I turn my back
on the hills
all I see is our farm

rising rising
to the crest of the escarpment
down down threaded

creek beds
dry in autumn
but rushing, teeming in the spring rains

generations husband the land
grandfather to father
father to son

unless
there are no sons
for the legacy of land

daughters belong to fathers
then husbands
with no right to the land

but land is in our blood
our blood is in the land
which knows no difference

some are nomads by choice
following pasture
following water

Bedouin wealth bound in carpets
Mongolian herders roll up yurts of skins
Kalahari people range far and wide

some seek a home
a place to belong
a place steeped within you

this is the land
the land in you impossibly
bound and wound within

where is home when the land
which freely took from you
is taken away from you

what is left
homeless, adrift in the world
seasons passing unmarked

pointless passing fields
watching skies, rising early
to greet an office

remember
black loam sifting through your fingers
land that was once yours

some days
I think I'll return
to the farm which isn't mine

walk the fence-lines if they remain
goldenrod and sumac turning
brilliant jewels of the waning autumn

I no longer count
the years of my youth
spent on the land

perhaps in the silver of my winter
I'll find a small bit of land to call my own
leave it to seed, weeds waving in the wind

once more turn my back
see that all in my view is mine
belong to the land once more

before the soil
like sands of time
sifts through my fingers

Albert Wong

Beyond Illusory Space #003

Watercolor on Paper

24 in x 34 in

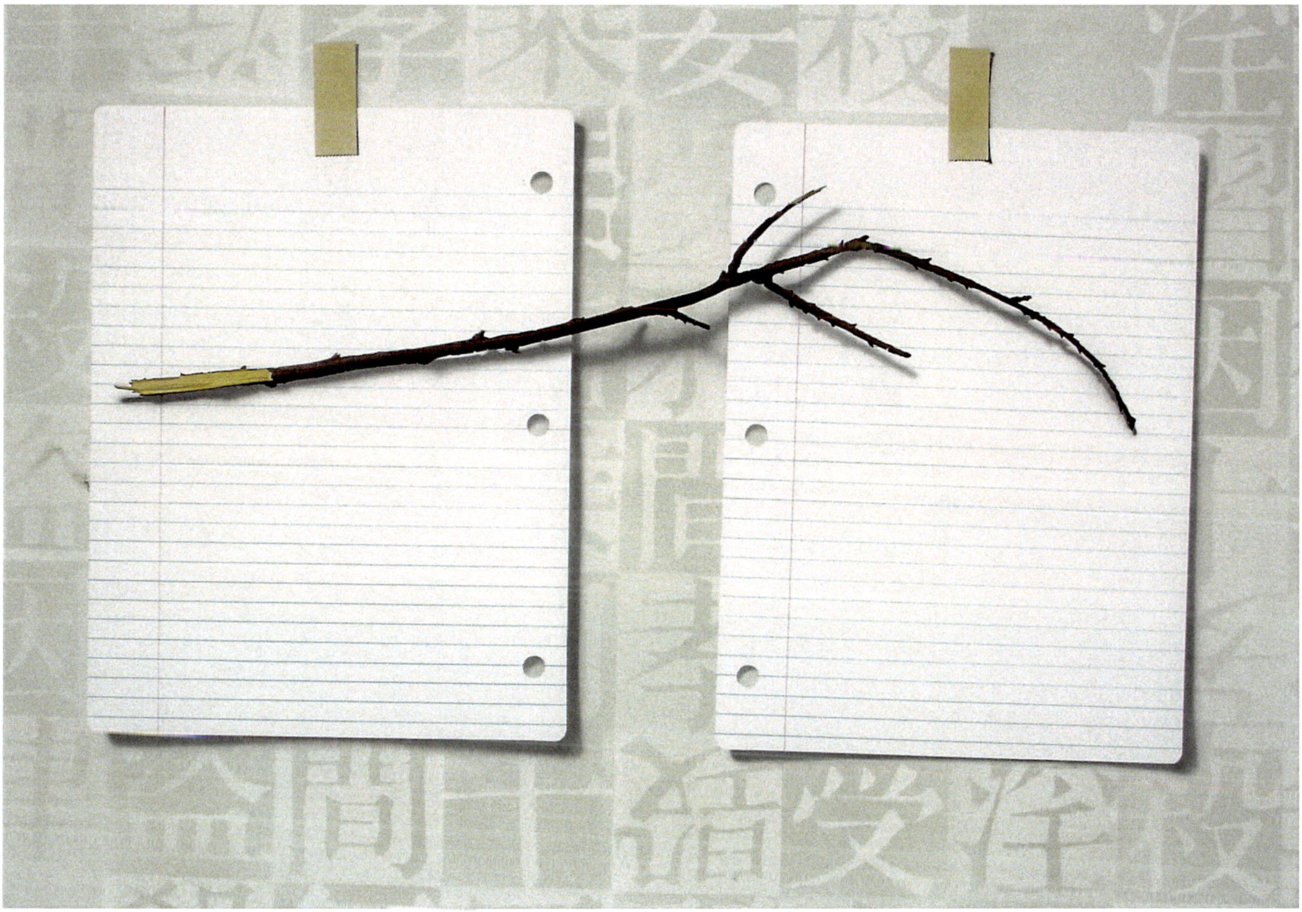

Albert Wong

Beyond Illusory Space #020

Watercolor on Paper

46 in x 34 in

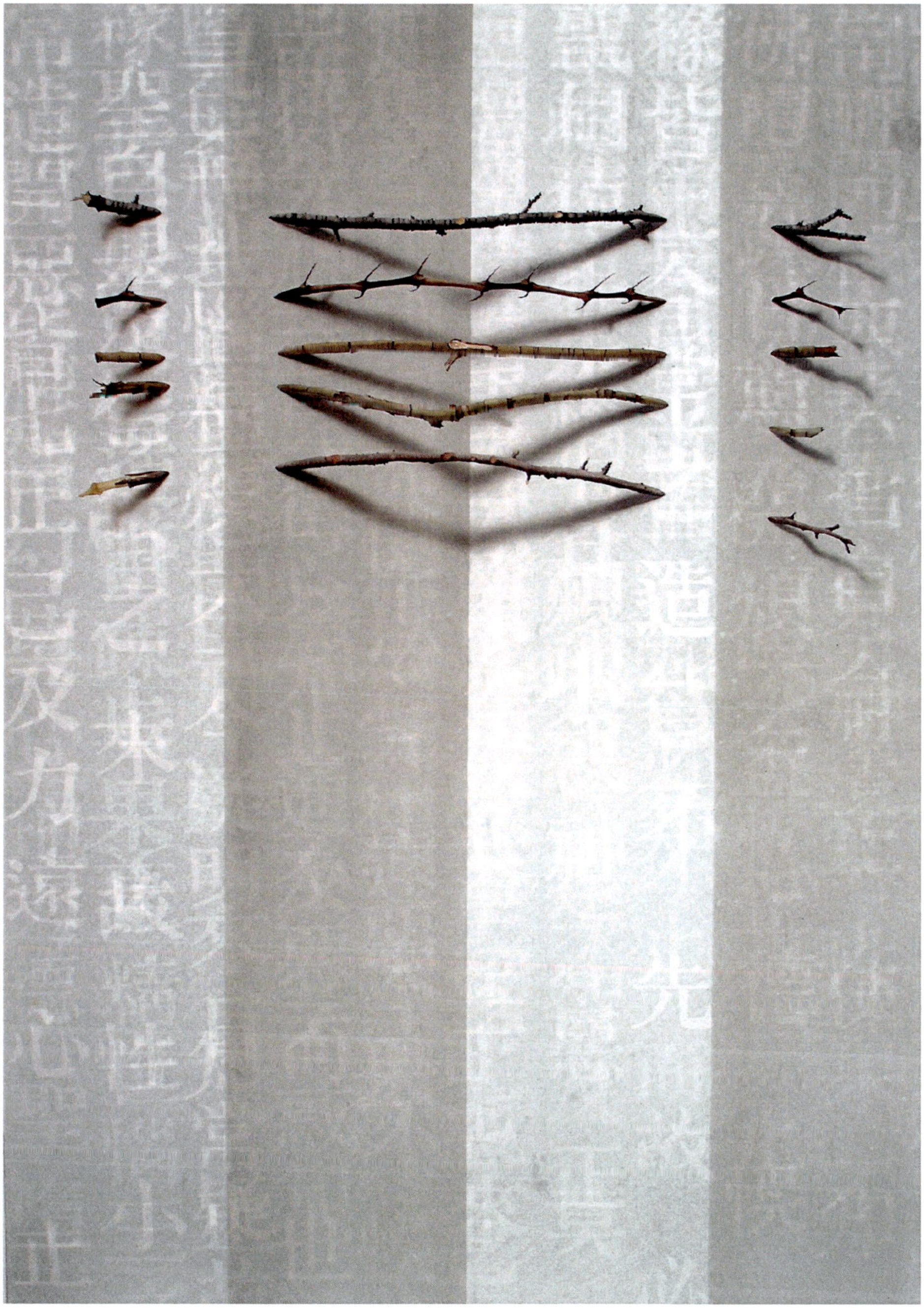

Albert Wong

Beyond Illusory Space #011

Watercolor on Paper

14.75 in x 10.5 in

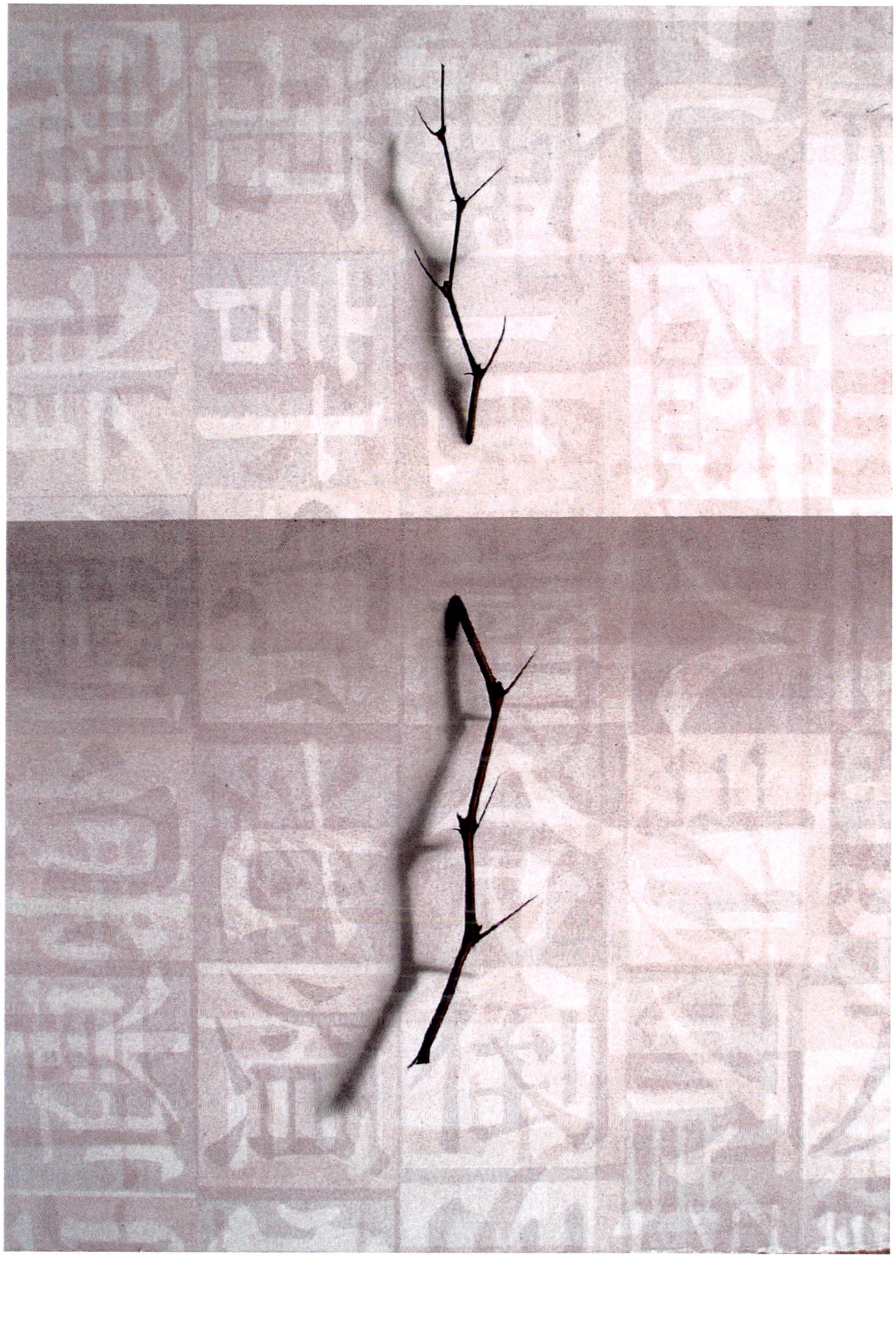

Debbie Crawford

Yuletide Tapestry

Watercolor

8 in x 10 in

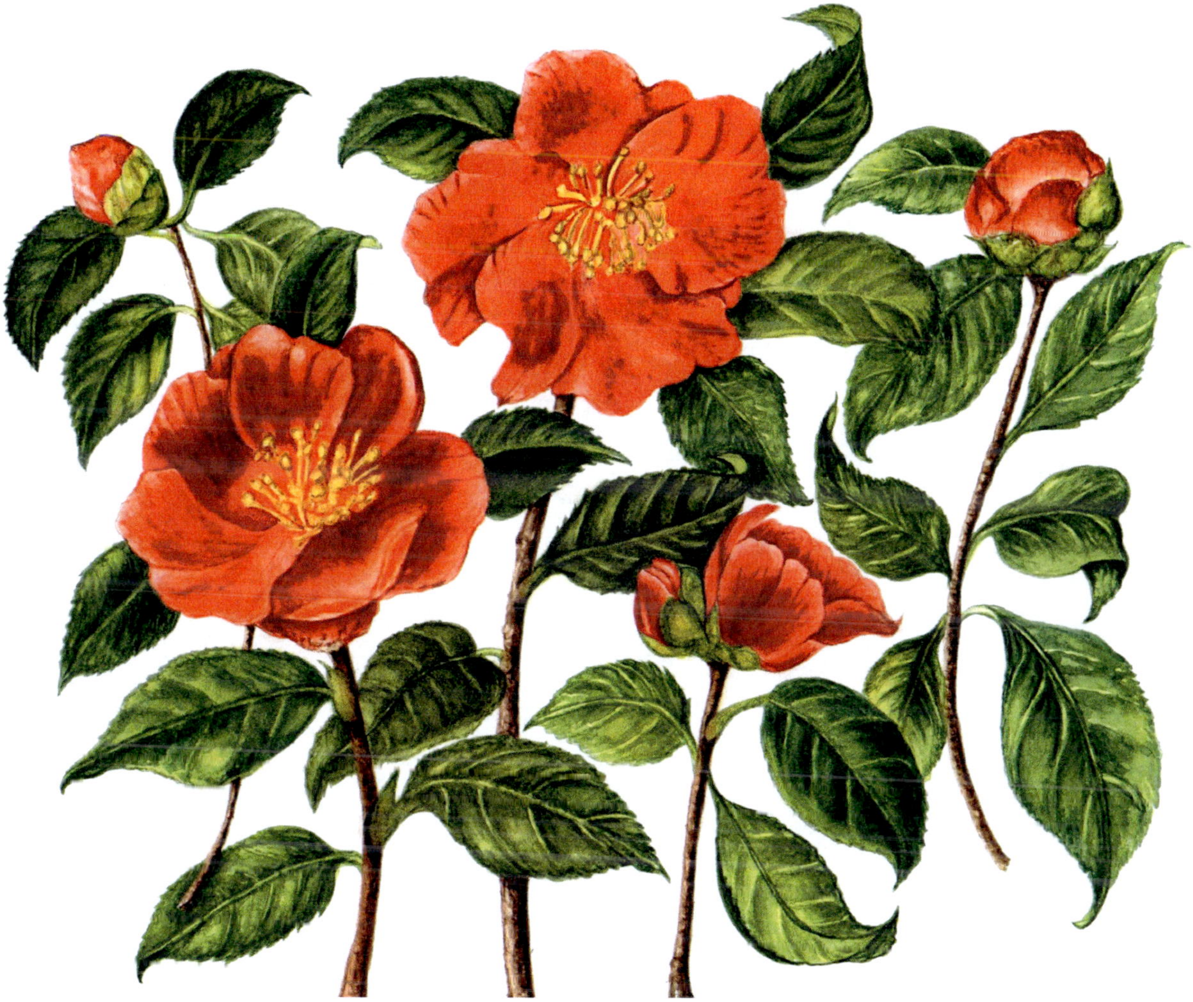

Debbie Crawford

Winter's Joy

Watercolor

8 in x 10 in

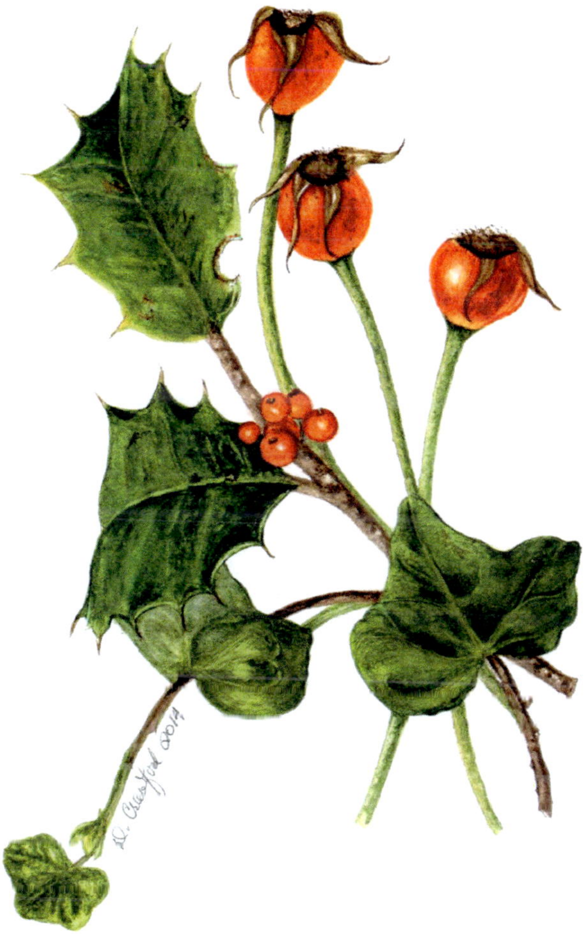

Rhonda Denney

Winter Early Morning LIght

Fiber Art

12 x 12 in

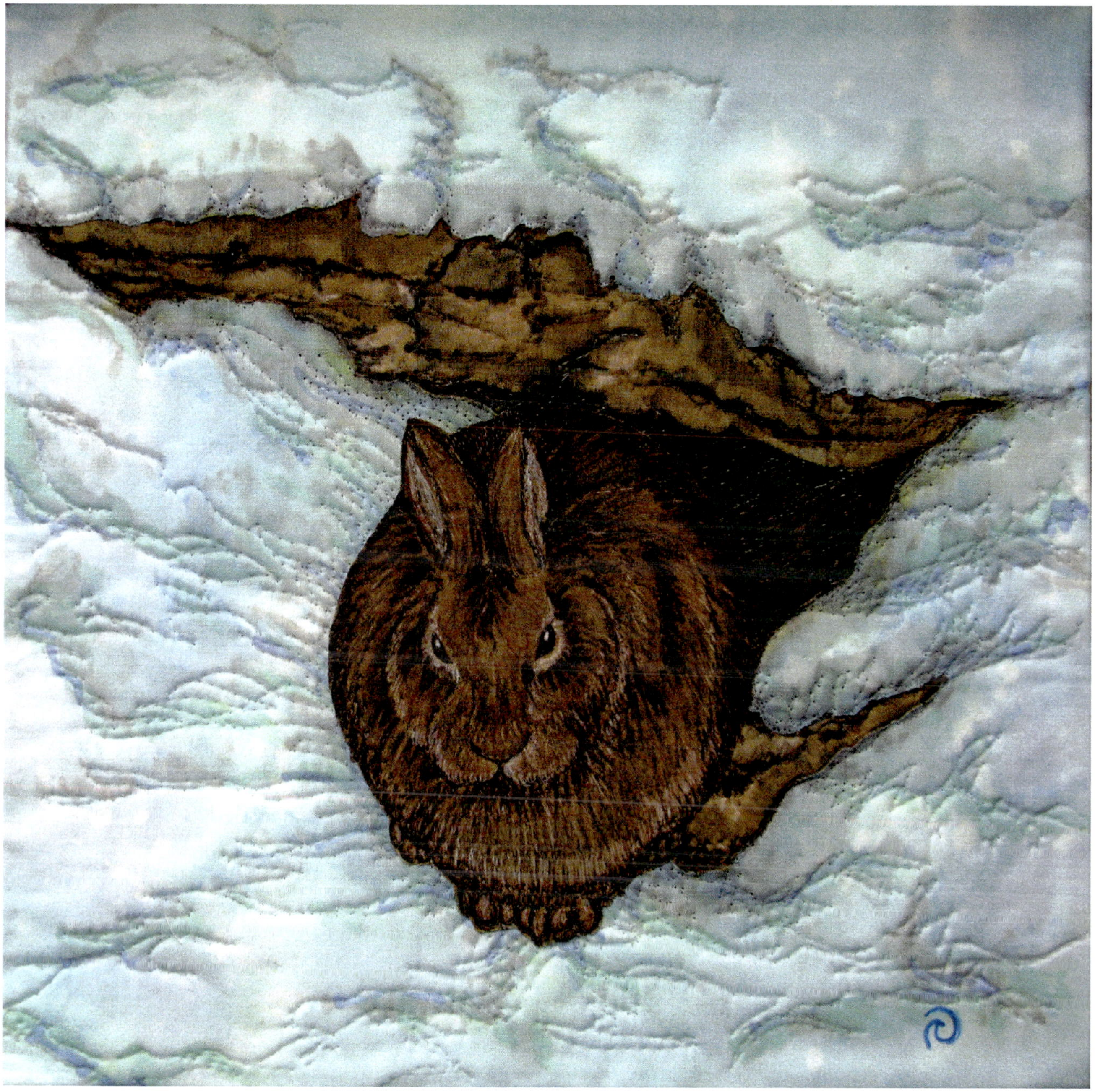

Charolte Mullich

Red Berries

Watercolor

12 in x 18 in

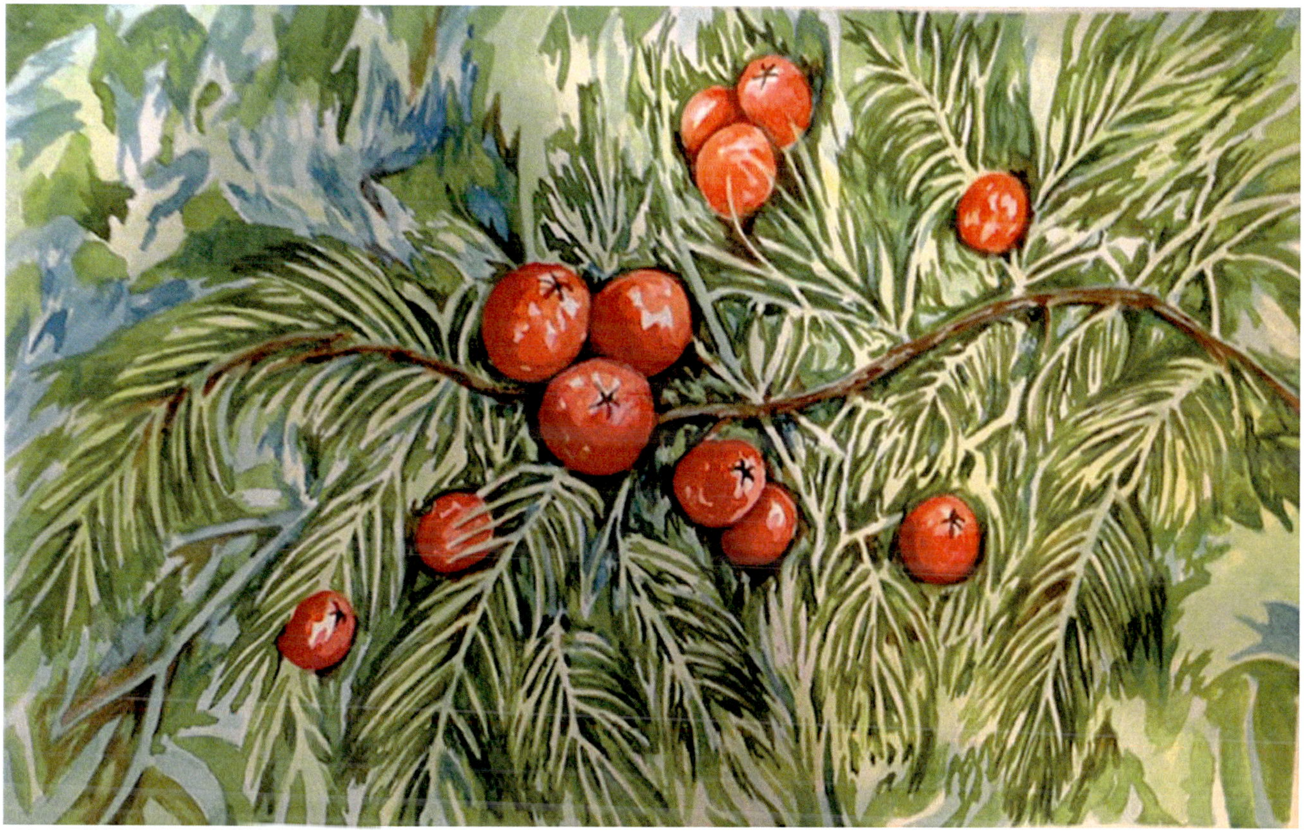

Night Sky

By Pamela Herron

skeletal branches
scratch at the window sighing
whispering winter

brittle fingers tap
wind rustles leaves underfoot
silken skirts dancing

black limbs scar the moon
calligraphy of heaven
brushed by a crow's wing

Kyung Eun You

She, Lost

Etching

4 in x 5.25 in

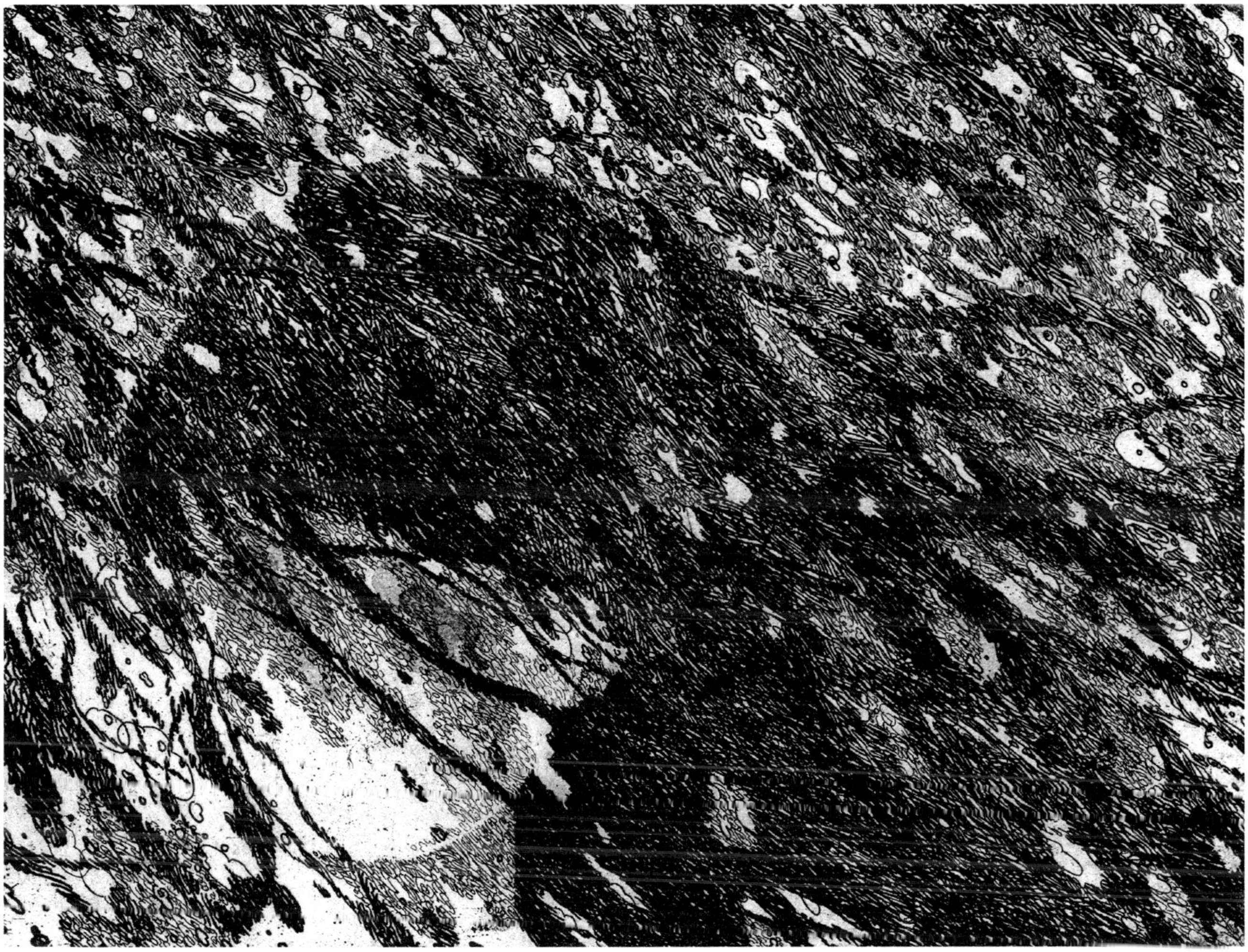

Kyung Eun You

She, Lost II

Etching

4.5 in x 5.25 in

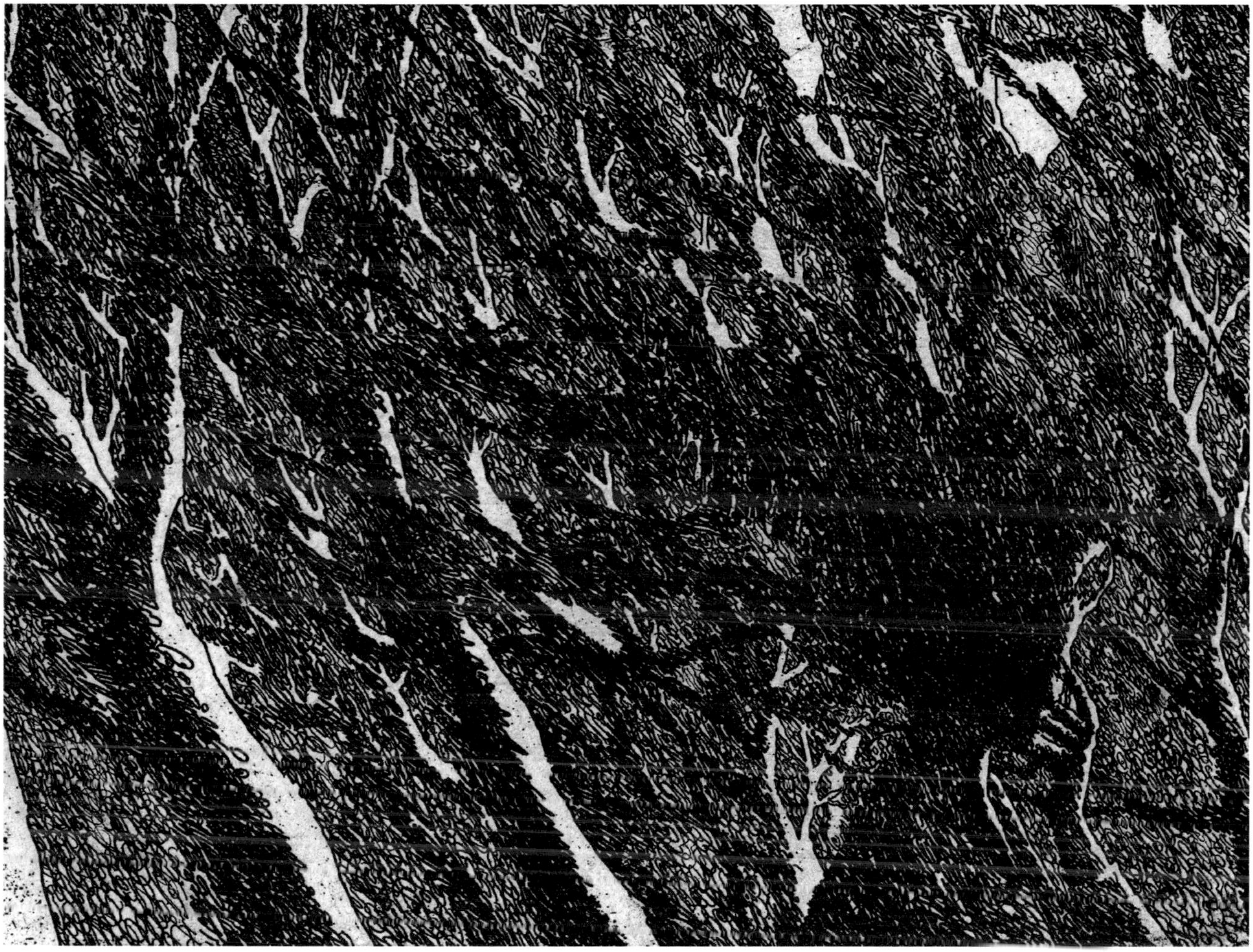

Olga Lebedeva

The Moon

Canvas Panel, Ink, Wine,
Original Poem

60 in x 48 in

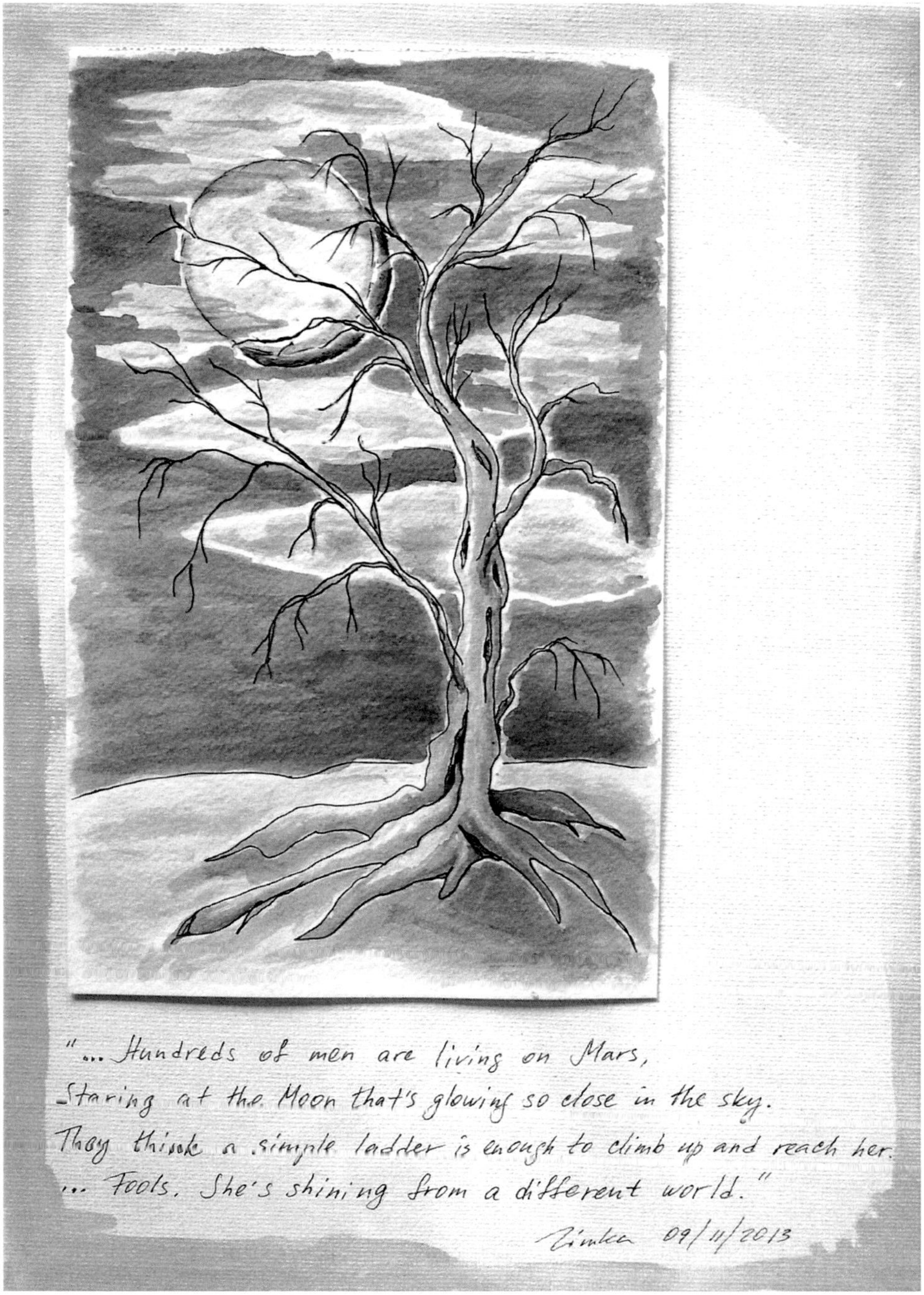
"... Hundreds of men are living on Mars,
Staring at the Moon that's glowing so close in the sky.
They think a simple ladder is enough to climb up and reach her.
... Fools. She's shining from a different world."
Zimka 09/11/2013

Olga Lebedeva

Beneath the Surface

Canvas, modeling paste, bugs, poppy seeds, thread, epoxy

4 in x 12 in x 3 in

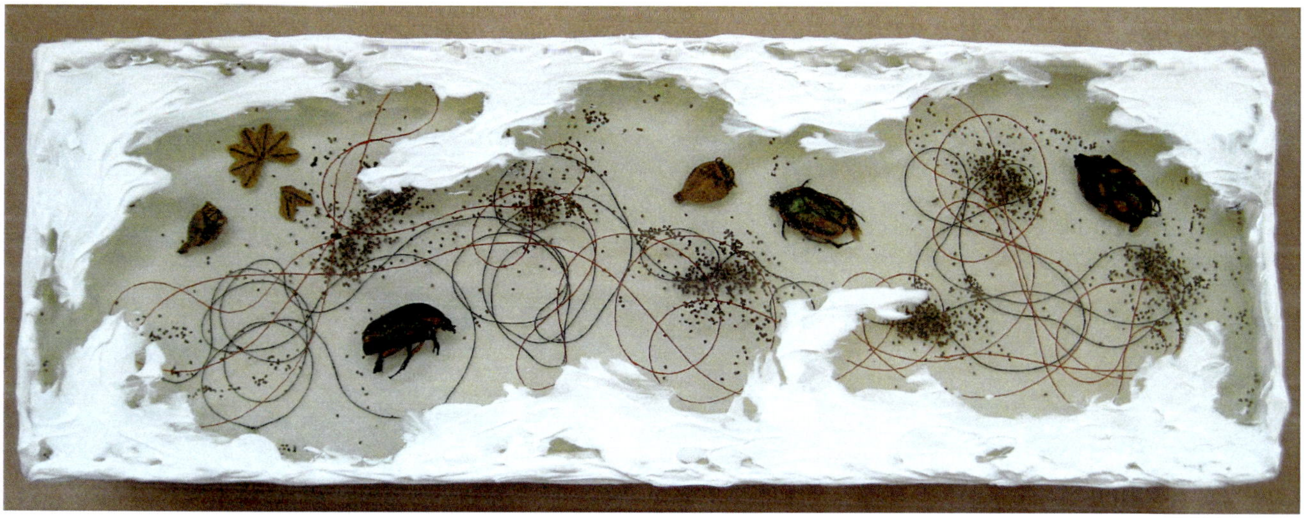

Tania Beaudet

East of the Sun and West of the Moon
Encaustic

24 in x 24 in

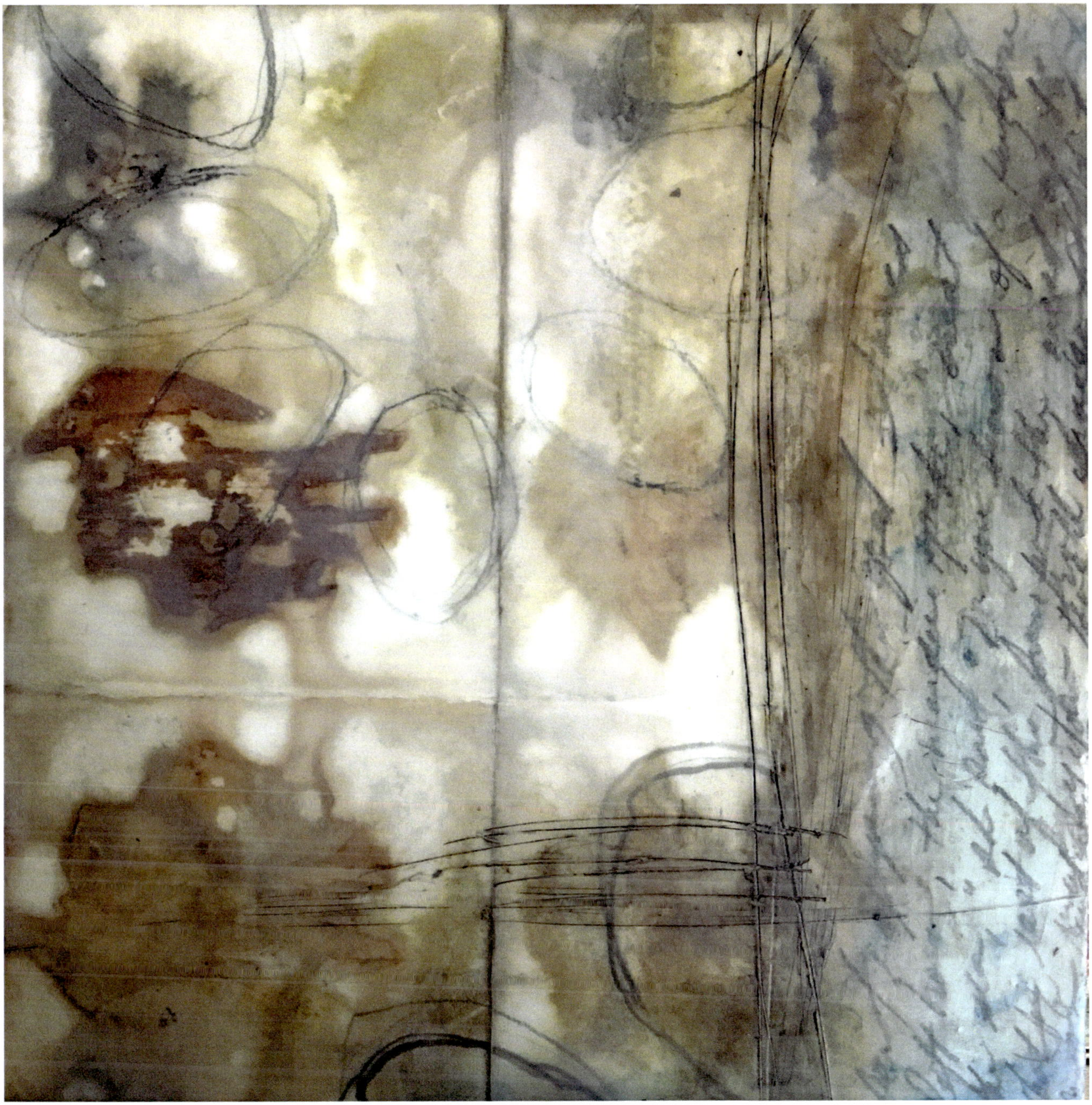

Tania Beaudet

4th Spectrum

Encaustic

24 in x 24 in

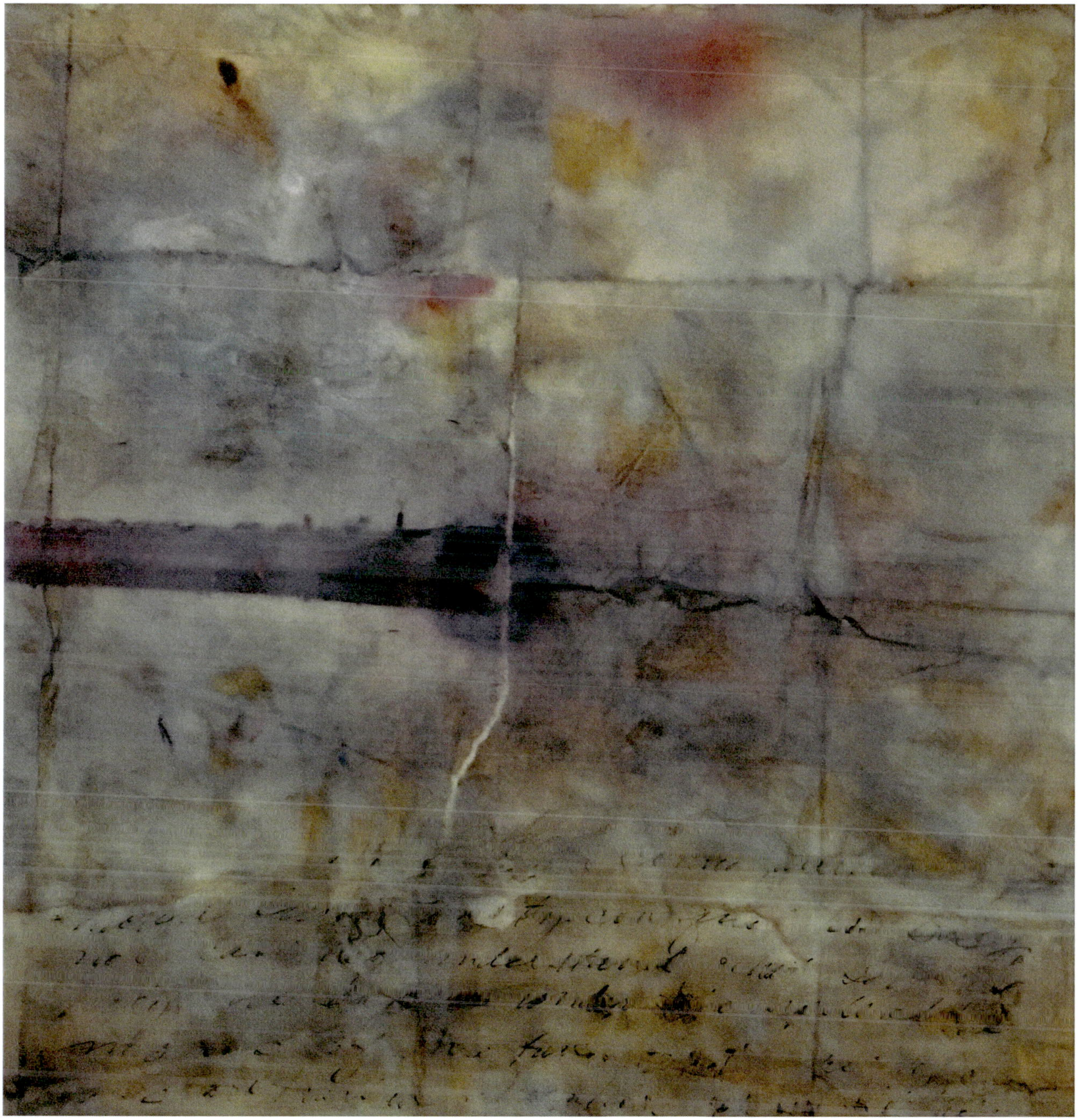

Hardie Cobbs

Stones of Stockholm

Painting

60 in x 48 in

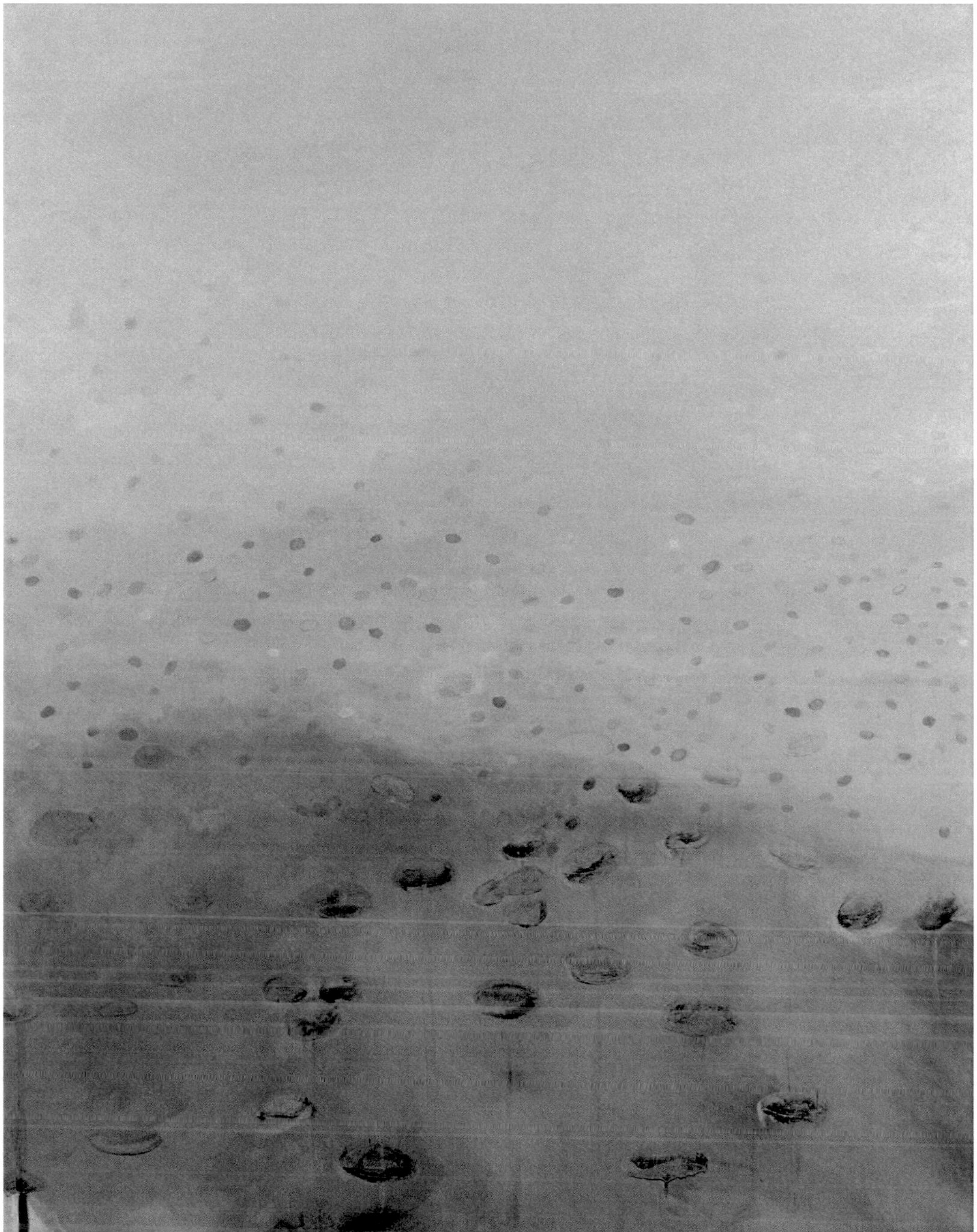

Winter Storm Watch

By Jeanne Julian

Hyped for nights,
this storm remains
restrained. Instead
of howling, only
sleet plectra on screens,
articulating potential,
typical precipitate
licks after entreaties
to brace for lashings
unprecedentedly relentless,
obliterating visible distinction
between mound and hollow,
justifying us as housebound.

Pent but teased
we must not give in
to indolence,
build-up or fizzle
being indeterminate still.
The mind drifts
to alternatives. It’s March.
We’re supposed to want
waking, not oblivion,
in this end-season.
But my mullioned view
of sunless sky surrendering
to frigid twilight, holding
its breath, turning blue, turns
me against lucidity:
bunkered, surrendering.
Release in no egress.

Jeanne Julian

Elusive

Photograph

11 in x 17 in

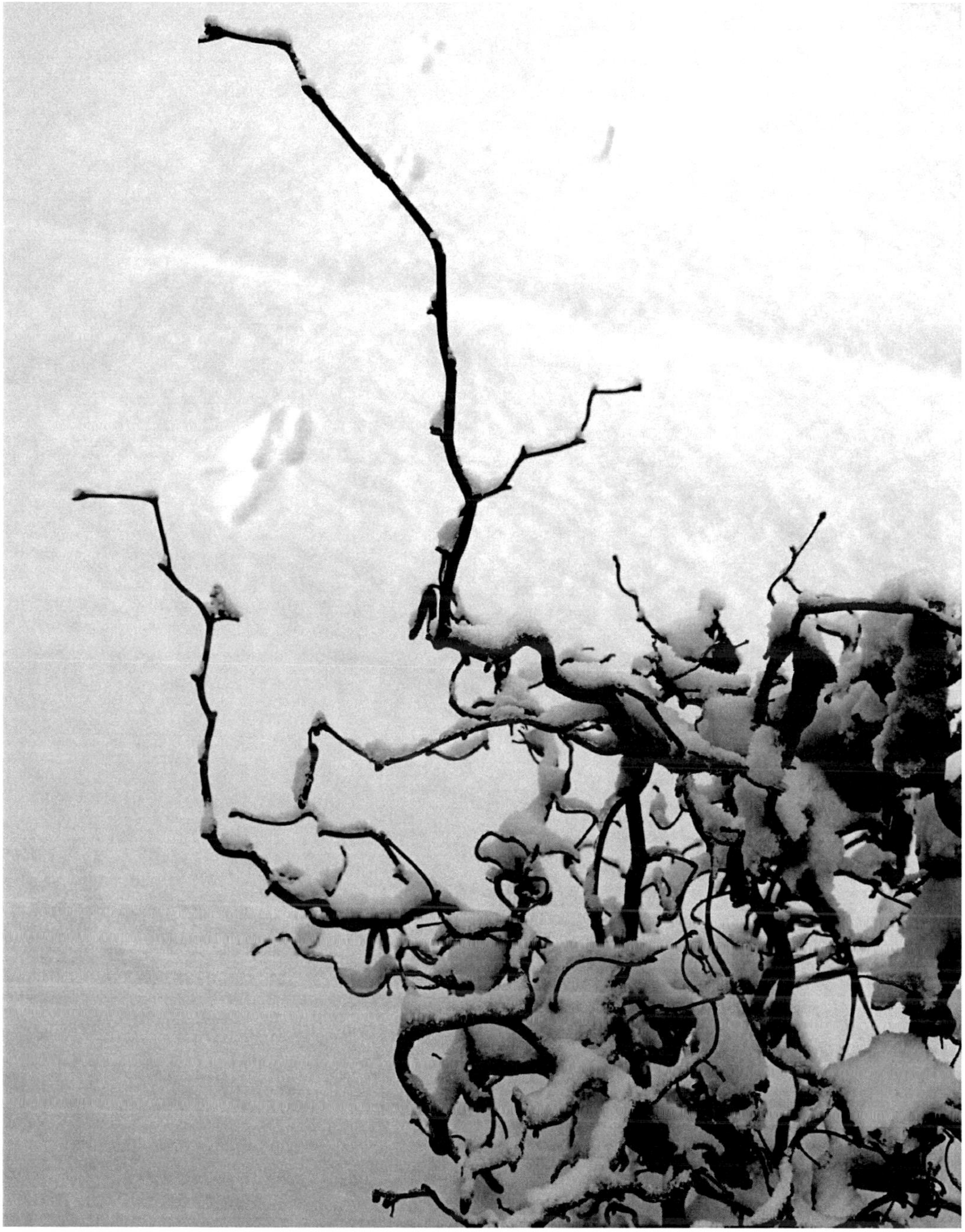

Jeanne Julian

Snow in the Croatan

Photograph

11 in x 17 in

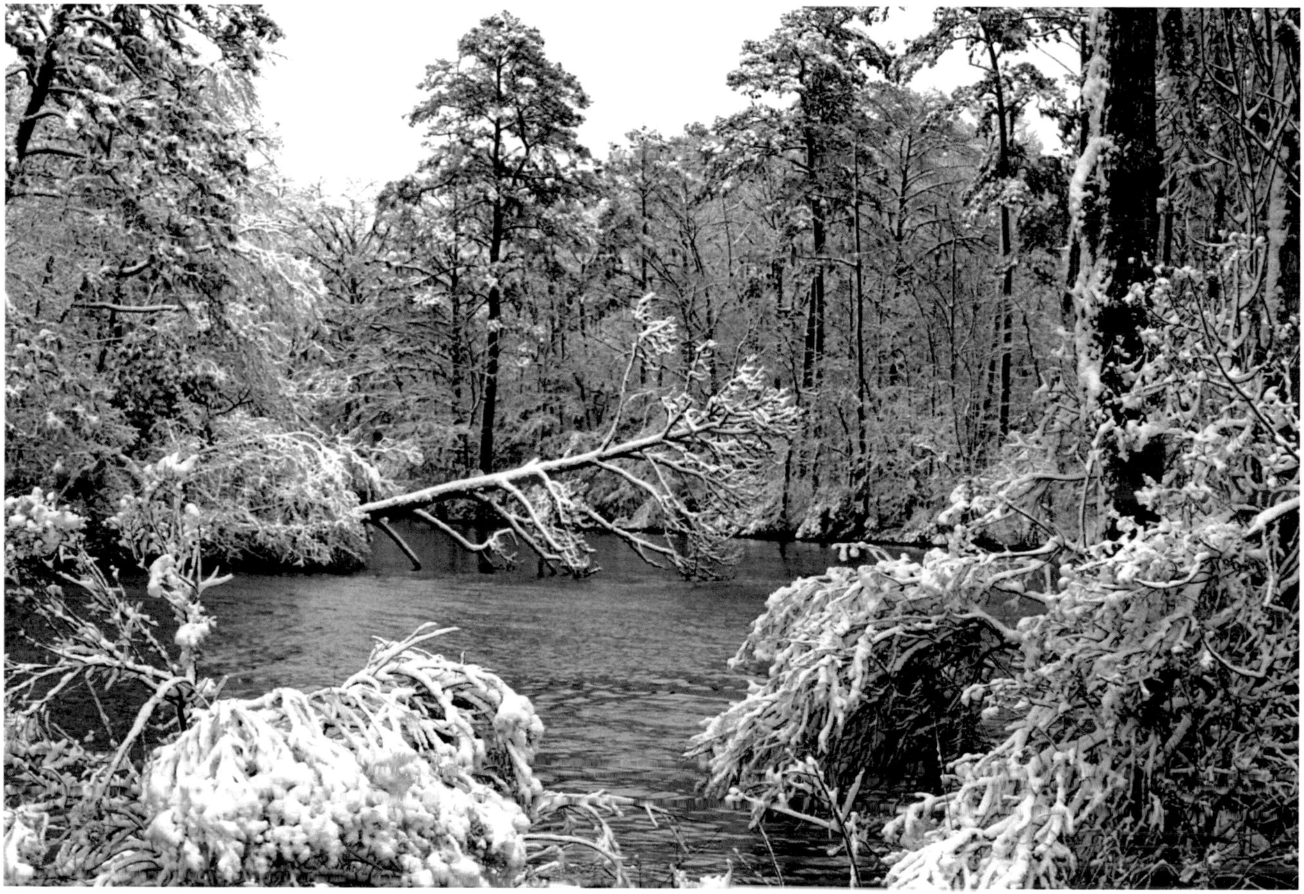

Jeanne Julian

Winter on Brices Creek

Photograph

16 in x 20 in

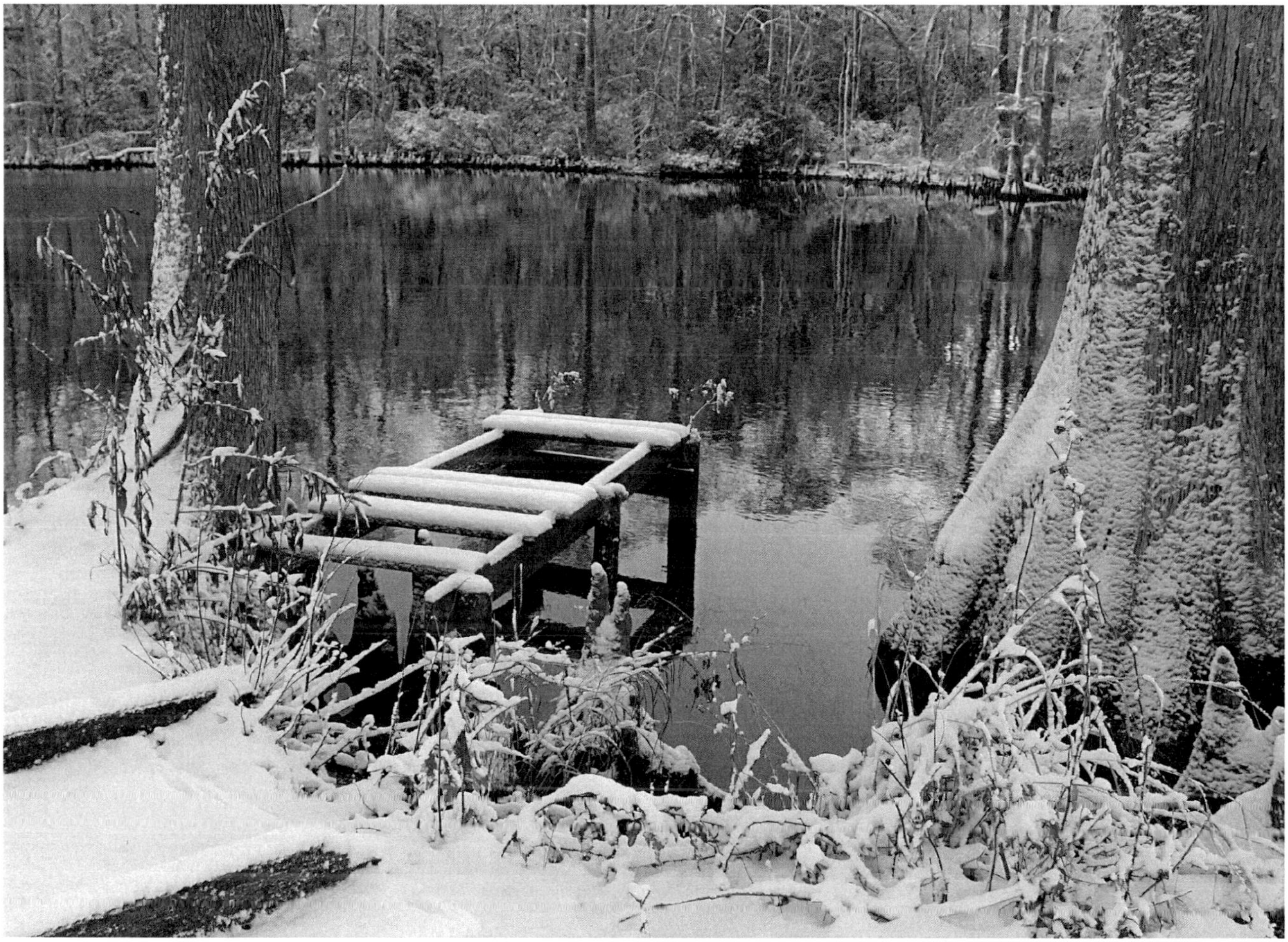

Jeanne Julian

Waiting for Spring

Photograph

11 in x 17 in

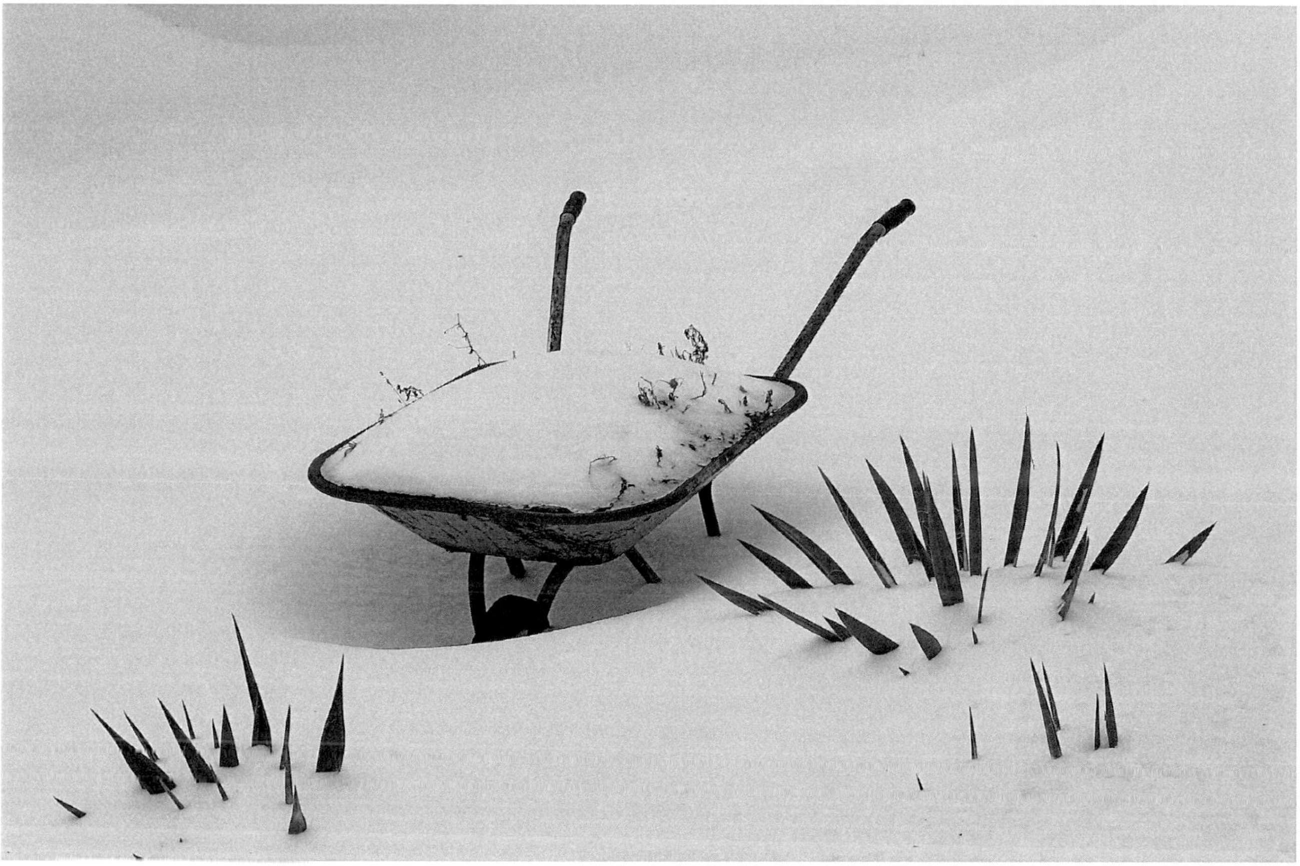

INDEX

Nature Inspired

Upcoming Editions

Spring 2016
Summer 2016
Autumn 2016
Winter 2016

Visit www.natureinspiredanthologies.com

Purchase a subscription and receive all four seasonal editions. Enter the call for art and writing to be included in future editions.

Find it all at the Nature Inspired Anthologies website site and join us on facebook at www.facebook.com/natureinspiredseries

28024399R00118

Made in the USA
Middletown, DE
29 December 2015